TURNAROUND

How
Carlos
Ghosn
Rescued
Nissan

HarperBusiness
An Imprint of HarperCollinsPublishers

TURN
AROUND

David
Magee

HarperCollins books may be purchased for educational, business, or sales promotional use. For information please write: Special Markets Department, HarperCollins Publishers Inc., 10 East 53rd Street, New York, NY 10022.

FIRST EDITION

Designed by William Ruoto
Photographs © Nissan North America

Library of Congress Cataloging-in-Publication Data
Magee, David.
    Turnaround : how Carlos Ghosn rescued Nissan / David Magee.—1st ed.
        p. cm.
    ISBN 0-06-051485-X
    1. Nissan Motor Corporation in U.S.A.—Management. 2. Automobile industry and trade—United States—Management. 3. Automobile industry and trade—Japan—Management. 4. Corporate turnarounds—United States. 5. Ghosn, Carlos, 1954– I. Title.

HD9710.U54 N555 2003
338.7'62922'092—dc21

                                                                    2002035745

03 04 05 06 07 ❖/QW 10 9 8 7 6 5 4 3 2 1

For my wife.

Acknowledgments

Many people contributed to the development of this book but nobody played a bigger role than Carlos Ghosn, who made himself and his company completely accessible to the author and made it clear that no subjects were off limits.

Dozens of others at Nissan at all levels of the company contributed significantly to the project by digging up requested facts and information and arranging interviews in Tokyo; Los Angeles; Smyrna, Tennessee; and La Jolla, California. Among them are Debra Sanchez Fair, Terri Hines, Keiko Tanaka, Kiho Ohga, and Gina Pasco.

This book would not have happened without my literary agent, Elizabeth Frost Knappman of New England Publishing Associates. She knows publishing inside and out and represents her authors with a passion, to say the least.

A special thank you to my editor, David Conti of Harper Business. It is doubtful there is anyone who knows the business of business books better than he does.

Others at HarperBusiness who deserve acknowledgment

for their hard work and efforts on behalf of this project include Lisa Berkowitz, one of the best in the book marketing business; Kristin Ventry, who sold foreign rights literally before the ink was dry on my contract; Sarah Love; and Knox Huston.

Others who played significant roles in roundabout ways include Dr. Will Norton, who taught me years ago there are many good stories to tell—tell them; Robyn Tannehill, a good friend who always recognizes opportunity; and L. A. Magee, for patiently reading the manuscript during its development phase.

Preface

When I first began working on this book about multicultural business executive Carlos Ghosn and his turnaround effort at Nissan I was struck by the frequency with which one word continually surfaced.

The word is transparency. As in, we have nothing to hide and consumers and shareholders will always be given a clear, unobstructed view of our company.

I was intrigued by this fresh talk and idea that a company viewed transparency as being critical to its long-term success. Then came the troubles of Enron and Kenneth Lay and WorldCom and Bernie Ebbers, and it was obvious to me this is a story that Americans, as well as the rest of the world, needed to hear.

All big business in the world is not being conducted in the same manner. And that, above all, served as my inspiration for this book.

More than two dozen top-level Nissan executives (including Ghosn) were interviewed. Many were longtime Japanese executives not accustomed to in-depth interviews with Western journalists. Yet, they, too, recognized this was a story that needed to be told, and cooperated by providing details of how it happened, problems that were encountered, and techniques that were used.

The result, I hope, is a book that tells an interesting global business story, while revealing the specifics of a new, international management style used by Carlos Ghosn and Nissan.

—*David Magee*

Contents

TURNAROUND

CHAPTER ONE

Breaking New Ground (Spring 2001)

Every few minutes another bus emerges from a dust cloud and stops, unloading dignitaries by the dozens. They are dressed the same: men in blue suits, women in high heels. But they are different. Some are black; some white; others Japanese, creating a cultural mix rarely seen in these parts in large numbers. It's a sunny spring day in rural Canton, Mississippi, and hundreds have come to hear the words of a fiery, intellectual, Brazilian-born, French-educated man of Lebanese descent, Carlos Ghosn.

Nissan Motor Company is breaking ground for its new $930 million North American manufacturing plant. The plant is an integral part of the revival plan designed to return to greatness the company that struggled so badly in the late 1990s that insiders feared the doors might close due to a lack of sustained profitability and industry leadership. Ghosn, at this time the company's president and chief operating officer, is on hand for the honors. So are other dignitaries one would expect at such an event, including Mississippi governor Ronnie Musgrove, who earned Ghosn's trust and was a leading factor in the plant-location decision. It's a moment of celebration for Mississippi, a state at or near the bottom of most economic rankings.

Mississippi has seen better times of late, certainly, thanks to money flowing from water-based gambling, which was approved by the state legislature ten years ago. Mississippi recently eclipsed New Jersey, becoming the country's second largest gambling state behind Nevada, but few noticed outside the gaming industry. There have been other successes. WorldCom, based in Clinton, became a telecommunications giant in the 1990s as CEO Bernie Ebbers engineered a string of leveraged acquisitions that for a time, before its fall, inflated stock portfolios of baby boomers throughout the sparsely populated state and created better-paying jobs. Mississippi was also the place that attacked the nation's tobacco companies and won, making a handful of the state's lawyers rich.

Still, most of the attention given to Mississippi goes to other things, like its storied and troubled racial past, or the high infant mortality rate, or the Confederate stars and bars that still adorn the state flag. It is a proud place, to be sure, but one that rarely celebrates victory over other states, much less its Southern neighbors. Tennessee landed Saturn in Spring Hill and Nissan in Smyrna; Alabama got Mercedes-Benz in Vance.

Governor Ronnie Musgrove told Nissan officials seeking a North American plant location in 2000 that it was his state's turn to land an automaker. He solicited help from Senator

Trent Lott and persuaded the state's legislature to offer incentives so rich—$295 million—Nissan couldn't say no. Canton is one of the poorer towns in one of the poorer states, but those factors did not matter to Nissan. So here is Ghosn, in unfamiliar territory, waiting patiently on stage for the groundbreaking ceremony to begin.

Mississippi is about to take a statewide vote on adopting a new flag, minus the Confederate reminders on the current one, and public debate over the issue has been sharing headlines with the announcement of the Nissan plant. Polls show the anticipated vote runs deeply down racial lines. And local wisdom, like the polls, says the new look has no chance of passing.

Almost forty years have passed since James Meredith integrated Ole Miss, Mississippi's flagship university, to the dismay of then-governor Ross Barnett and thousands of citizens who protested his federally mandated enrollment. Blood was shed and lives were lost, but Meredith, flanked by thousands of National Guard troops dispatched by President John F. Kennedy, enrolled at and later graduated from the University. Today more than 1,000 African American students attend Ole Miss and tunes of racial harmony have been sung there and throughout the state in recent years by the likes of Myrlie Evers, the wife of slain civil rights leader Charles Medger Evers, and actor Morgan Freeman, who lives in rural northwest Mississippi. The flag—a last remaining symbol of white traditionalists—is another story.

But Mississippi's past is being displaced by a unified future on this day. The sun is bright and the temperature is cool inside the big-top tent and a diverse group is assembling inside to watch Ghosn, an emerging world business leader, officially announce the coming of a Japanese corporation to Mississippi.

The all-black Canton High School band plays. A Japanese "Taiko" drum corps is on hand to stir the crowd and remind all that Nissan is still steeped in its home country's traditions. A nearby resident says the event is "a blessing from God." It's also unity.

Ghosn speaks. He talks about Nissan's revival efforts and affirms the company's return to profitability for a full fiscal year, a far cry from the brink of bankruptcy it had faced two years earlier. He says Nissan will employ thousands at the Mississippi plant and make new products, giving the company a bigger presence and brighter future in America.

"Building the right products in the right markets is a basic ingredient to building a foundation for solid profitable growth," Ghosn said. "And that is exactly what we are doing here. Nissan's investment in Canton is a key part of that foundation.

"The Canton plant will produce a full-size pickup truck, a full-size sport-utility vehicle, and the next-generation Nissan minivan. This is a significant and critical expansion of our lineup in the U.S. market," Ghosn said. "It will allow us to increase our responsiveness to the market, decrease our costs, and reduce our exposure to currency fluctuations."

A black lady wearing a Sunday dress is half-seated on a table at the rear of the tent and waving her arms. She punctuates every word of emphasis and pause from Ghosn loud and clear with words of thanksgiving: *"Praise God."*

For Mississippi, it's an amen day. Up to 4,000 high-wage jobs, a billion dollar-investment . . . unity. For Nissan and

Ghosn, it's a parlay play of an aggressive revival plan designed to return Nissan to its position as one of the most respected and (in some circles) feared automakers in the world.

A Company with Tradition

Nissan was established in Japan in 1933. It made a major impact on the global auto market in the late 1950s when it first introduced its Datsun brand sedans and compact pickup trucks to the United States. It was a risky move coming so soon after World War II when negative emotions toward the Japanese still ran high in some corners, but the products didn't appeal to older Americans loyal to General Motors anyway. The sports cars were sleek and exactly what the younger, faster generation wanted. The 2000 Roadster, with its five-speed, 150-horsepower engine, was first produced in 1967, establishing the Datsun brand as a symbol of unique European style and Japanese performance.

The company experienced dramatic growth in the 1970s when its popular Z model was introduced. The 240Z became the fastest selling sports car in the world, selling more than 500,000 units in fewer than ten years. The long-nosed rocket car, desired by teenagers and twenty-somethings across America, helped push Nissan's other Datsun products to popularity as well, positioning the brand in America as one with unequaled performance, engineering, and value.

By 1975 Datsun was the top U.S. vehicle importer and Nissan's Japanese style of business was well documented—and envied—throughout the world, particularly in the United States where General Motors and Chrysler struggled with antiquated management, too slow to react to the invigorated, fast-moving Japanese, who produced cars with a quality and efficiency unheard of in the United States.

Nissan opened its first U.S. plant in Smyrna, Tennessee, in 1983, producing the small Datsun pickup truck, which sold hundreds of thousands of units for the company. Two years later the company was making the compact Sentra in Smyrna, and the company began marketing all of its vehicles worldwide under the Nissan name. The company launched its luxury Infiniti line in 1989, capping a decade of success in the United States and North America. Sales in the United States peaked at 830,767 cars and small trucks sold in 1985 and, although the number fluctuated at slightly lower levels through the 1990s, the importance Nissan placed on North American sales increased as sales in Japan declined year after year.

Serious problems developed at Nissan in the early 1990s. Management once hailed as progressive and trend-setting was now a part of Japan's old-boy network, arrogant and oblivious to market changes and customer needs. A classic example: instead of reinventing the once-popular Z car when sales declined, management chose to let volume fall and defer a redesigned model, putting in limbo a crucial element of the company's global identity. At the heart of the problem were Japanese business tradition and the conservative style of Nissan managers. Top Japanese companies are often tied together through traditional supplier relationships—"keiretsu," a system of cross-holding of stocks that was devised during the country's rapid economic growth in the 1950s and 1960s.

Typically, 30 to 50 percent of stocks in Japanese corporations are cross-held by companies in the same keiretsu as a means of preventing takeovers by outside investors and promoting profits among allies.

In sectors such as automobile manufacturing, this process fostered long-term relationships between buyers and suppliers, as keiretsu members worked together on product development. Nissan was deeply tied into this process because senior management felt obligated to buy from its group partners, typically at a premium. Simply stated, suppliers over time had raised prices to the point that Tokyo-based Nissan could do nothing but struggle. Former Nissan chairman Yoshifumi Tsuji admitted in 1999 that the company's problems were far worse than anticipated, saying that this Japanese practice of cross-holding stocks was a liability to Nissan and other companies in Japan.

Nissan had many other problems as well. The fact that the company was in dire straits was no secret, but nobody in Japan had a solution, since it was considered taboo in the country for these keiretsu links to be broken. Eventually Nissan was strapped by $22 billion in debt, inflated supplier costs, and new product development that was at a standstill. Once-generous financiers were tightening the noose on the company. Nissan was on the brink of bankruptcy, its stock price drifting lower, and executives were holding merger discussions with other automakers.

Dealers in key markets like the United States had sparse lots and were only able to sell the U.S.-produced Sentra and small pickups with any volume—products that had virtually no profit margin for the dealer or for Nissan. And at home, in Japan, the company that once owned more than one third of its domestic market now held less than 20 percent, suffering more than a quarter century of market share decline.

Looking for a Savior

Mergers were the flavor of the day in the automotive industry, the largest and most notable being Daimler-Benz and Chrysler, and almost every carmaker worldwide was looking left and right for potential partners. Nissan, the conservative Japanese company with the rising sun as part of its corporate logo, was openly courting suitors, holding serious discussions with the likes of the new DaimlerChrysler and Ford Motor Company. But Ford's Jacques Nasser and Chrysler's Robert Eaton and Thomas Stallcamp scoffed at the move after exploratory meetings.

Ghosn, an executive vice president at Renault, felt differently, to say the least. He had a vision different than others and wanted Renault to take a hard look at the ailing Japanese company. Renault, under the leadership of CEO Louis Schweitzer, was fresh off its own recovery, stronger than ever before, but much smaller than what Nissan management originally had in mind in terms of a suitor. Still, Schweitzer, Ghosn, and others at Renault sensed desperation in Japan and believed that faced with no options, powers-that-be in the country would not oppose French capital taking over the company regarded by many to be the centerpiece of Japan's postwar industrial success.

They couldn't have been more right. The Ministry of International Trade and Industry (MITI), now referred to as the Ministry of Economy, Trade, and Industry (METI), the powerhouse of the Japanese economy, publicly blessed the move and public sentiment in Japan was calm, even welcoming. The Renault-Nissan Alliance was formed and multicultural Carlos Ghosn, who had never before lived in Asia and did not speak Japanese, was named chief operating officer of a Japanese company.

"A lot of things characterize the Japanese people," Ghosn said. "We can debate them. But one characteristic we cannot debate is that they are very pragmatic. They are also very sensitive to reality. And the reality of Nissan was not hidden. It was crystal clear. Something had to be done."

The man charged with leading Japan's No. 3 automaker (Toyota is the largest, while Nissan and Honda flip-flop between the second and third positions) is a globalist who has traveled extensively as an upper level corporate executive, drawing his paycheck on four different continents in the past decade. He likes Rio de Janeiro, Paris, and Greenville, South Carolina—places he has lived during his international management stops.

Ghosn, in fact, may be the only person to have four verifiable corporate turnaround efforts on four different continents to his credit. Different languages were spoken at each place and the challenge was vastly different, allowing him to take elements from each of the diverse experiences and develop what has become a unique approach to international business management and corporate turnaround efforts. Ghosn sees business as a universal unifier of people because of its common goal factors and uses his ability to work across cultural lines to that end.

Le Cost Killer

When Ghosn was named Nissan's chief operating officer in 1999—the title of President was given in 2000; the CEO title in 2001—the challenge was monumental compared to what he had faced as leader-apprentice at Michelin South America (Brazil), Michelin North America (Greenville, South Carolina), and Renault (France). He was in charge at both regional Michelin operations and was one of a handful of executive vice presidents at Renault, but Nissan was the first company where all decisions, ultimately, were his.

"It is different when you are the one making the final decision," Ghosn says.

The company was about to go under when he arrived and it took all the training and experience he had from his days at Michelin and Renault to find ways to save Nissan. Many conventional management practices would not work in Japan due to general skepticism in the country about Western ways of doing business. So Ghosn used his experience to develop a style unique for Nissan and never wavered in his commitment to the tactics he used.

When Renault's Schweitzer announced in March 1999 that his company was taking a 36.8 percent stake in Nissan for $5.4 billion, and when it was announced three months later that Ghosn would take charge of the struggling company, more than a few in the global business community were surprised. It was one thing for Renault to take control of Nissan; it was another thing altogether for an outsider to be sent in so quickly. Few questioned whether a hardliner like Ghosn could create change at Nissan. They wondered if a Westerner would face crippling hostility and revolt from Japanese accustomed to a bureaucratic and slow-moving style steeped in a deep tradition of techniques once revered by business gurus everywhere.

The business challenge was one thing; the cultural challenge another.

Even if the people were accepting in the beginning, how would they react to massive changes long-term? Ghosn earned the nickname "le cost killer" in France for his drastic cost-cutting recommendations at Renault. It was no secret that Ghosn was a driving force behind Renault's controversial decision in the late 1990s to close a major manufacturing plant in Vilvoorde, Belgium. The Japanese economy was in bad shape already when Ghosn arrived and plant closings there certainly would be met with a revolt, a bruising local effort to put the foreigner in his rightful place—out of Japan.

Ghosn, however, arrived in Japan with an attitude oblivious to tradition and rolled the dice with his aggressive Nissan Revival Plan (NRP), announced October 1999. The plan was detailed and far-reaching, focusing on a quick return to profitability, debt reduction, and cost cutting while also creating long-term growth opportunities and setting the stage for explosive growth potential in the future. One result was the billion-dollar investment in the new Mississippi plant. That was the reason Ghosn wanted to see, experience, and understand the state in which Nissan would manufacture vehicles.

Granted, it's just one plant, but every move Ghosn has made to date has been geared at short-term survival and long-term consistency. The future—a growing, profitable future, that is—rests in part on Nissan's ability to produce innovative new products in America once again, reminiscent of the days in the 1960s and 1970s when the company changed the way people in the country viewed automobile engineering and manufacturing.

Ghosn acknowledges that Nissan is raising the stakes by investing so heavily in the future when current problems have yet to be fixed. Nissan is entering Mississippi to launch a new line of products, including the full-size pickup truck, that are viewed as risky by more than a few. Southerners love pickup trucks, but they have long-bred ties with Chevrolet and Ford; this is the reason Chevy's Silverado and Ford's F-150 series are the top-selling vehicles in America. In Mississippi, pickups are driven by doctors and lawyers and farmers and field hands and every professional and wage earner in between. The car in the driveway may be stamped Toyota or Nissan or BMW, but getting Southern drivers into a full-size pickup made outside of the Big Three is a full-size challenge.

But with a billion dollars down on the table in Mississippi, Ghosn isn't blinking, charging ahead in America with a mentality similar to that used by his Japanese predecessors at Nissan some fifty years earlier when they brought innovative sports cars and minivans to an American public used to buying predominantly from U.S. automakers.

"The challenge is big," he said at the time, "but we are coming from hell trying to get to purgatory. We have to make a difference and do it fast. New product is the key to the revival of Nissan. Our investment in the Canton, Mississippi, plant is a very important part of our future."

There is irony, of course, in the fact that Nissan's upward trek begins in a state still divided by its past. It isn't lost on

Ghosn, who learned quickly that traditions in the Magnolia State are held closely by many who are slow to change. Ghosn is undaunted, convinced about the strengths of the state he says will be another notch in an already strong American manufacturing presence.

And he is hoping that Mississippi, like Japan, is more adaptable to change than history and conventional wisdom suggest.

CHAPTER TWO

The Making of a New, International Leader

If anybody knows mismanagement, it's Carlos Ghosn. Each company he's worked for has been a textbook study in corporate misdirection, confusion, or both when he arrived . . . Michelin South America, Michelin North America, Renault, and now, Nissan.

He was CEO of Michelin North America, engineering that company's difficult acquisition of Uniroyal-Goodrich in the early 1990s, and an executive vice president of Renault, pushing for massive cost-cutting measures during that company's notable restructuring effort in the late 1990s. When he took control of Nissan he found a company that needed more than financial reform. The challenge began with restructuring the minds of thousands of employees who had lost confidence in the company and included the global unification of Nissan's ideas and operations.

Ghosn's dark hair and complexion, bushy eyebrows and bespectacled frame make stereotyping him difficult. He speaks four languages, is trying to learn a fifth—Japanese—and has lived and worked in Brazil, America, France, and Japan in recent years, absorbing the regional tastes and customs of each. He believes a country does not define a person and cultural boundaries are limitless if you are able to adapt while maintaining individual identity.

"Nationalities are not exclusive," Ghosn says. "You are not only what it says on your passport. National culture is additive . . . I belong to many countries, many environments. I find myself comfortable in Beirut [Lebanon], Greenville [South Carolina], Tokyo, Paris, and Rio de Janeiro. You simply add from one national culture to another. The more you add, the more you balance."

Ghosn believes that observing and learning from differences in others helps you create wealth in many ways.

A longtime friend and business associate says Ghosn learns quickly in each culture he is exposed to because he expects nothing more from the people than what he observes firsthand, ignoring negative stereotypes that plague people in all places. The differences offered by people and places in reality are what we should learn and take from. The assumption of others that Japanese businessmen will never change and that Mississippi is a state too far behind to be worth investing in is not enough for Carlos Ghosn, who recognizes each country and each culture on its own merits.

Ghosn was exposed to different cultures and global ways of thinking before entering the business world. His parents did not restrict the family to national boundaries or thoughts, teaching a young Carlos Ghosn the value of observing and learning from others in new places.

"He goes in quietly and learns from the people and places around him," says Jim Morton, who worked under Ghosn at Michelin North America in Greenville, South Carolina, and joined him in 2000 at Nissan as one of the top North American executives. "He stays very close to his family even though they live in different parts of the world. He never lets that go, but he adapts to new surroundings very easily."

A Close Family

Ghosn was born in Porto Velho, Brazil, on March 9, 1954, to Jorge and Rose Ghosn. Both are of Lebanese origin, though his mother had French citizenship, his father, Brazilian. Ghosn's father, like his father before him, worked in Brazil, running a portion of a family business. Jorge and Rose met when Jorge returned to Lebanon briefly to visit family and look for a woman to marry. Rose's family had an immigrant background as well, having moved from Lebanon to Nigeria, where her father ran an import-export business. Jorge and Rose married and returned to Brazil, where Jorge continued to run his business, assisting airlines with development in the remote Amazon region.

The second of four children, Carlos Ghosn was born in Brazil, but moved from Porto Velho to Rio de Janeiro with the entire family when he was just one or two years old when he became ill after drinking unsanitary water. When Ghosn was six, his mother moved her children to Lebanon. His father remained in Brazil to run his business, sending money home to the family. This long-distance arrangement was common for Lebanese families, the father earning a living in one country or region while the family lived in its native land. Despite the distance, though, Jorge played a major role in the everyday life of his family, returning home frequently for visits, fathering two more children, and instilling core values and strict discipline in his limited role.

"We might have lived apart," Ghosn says, "but we remained close as a family. This has a lot to do with the strong family bonds the Lebanese maintain with family members, regardless of where they might be living in the world. They place a high value on familial responsibilities—being a good father, being a good mother, being a good provider for the family. These . . . are deeply imbedded in the Lebanese culture."

The Troublemaker

Ghosn showed an exceptional knack for organization and focus even as a young man, excelling at Notre Dame College, the Jesuit school he attended in Lebanon for almost ten years. He was a problem at times, known for mischief and pranks, perhaps because his intellect, even then, allowed for boredom. But the young Ghosn spent hours with schoolwork until each problem, and ultimately each subject, was mastered. His older sister teased him, saying he must be tied to his desk. Once the work was done, though, he displayed an inability to accept mundane moments because of curiosity and a lack of patience.

"I was the first guy to cause trouble whenever I found an opportunity, especially when I was dissatisfied," Ghosn said. "If I thought the teacher was boring, I would disrupt the class with some kind of prank."

Ghosn was so well known for his intense personality, which led him to challenge authority and set off on new paths, that an inscription in his senior yearbook noted: *"Carlos Ghosn—the future leader of a guerrilla movement in South America."*

But more than pranks, Ghosn was known for excellence in the classroom. He felt driven by a competitive desire to learn more than those around him, or anywhere. And he eagerly absorbed a bigger picture from teachers who offered the eager-to-learn Ghosn nontextbook wisdom. One in particular, Father Lagrovole, gets credit from Ghosn for teaching some techniques the CEO uses in management.

- Be transparent and explain yourself in clear, lucid terms.
- Do as you say you are going to do.
- Listen first; then think.

Learning in France

Ghosn had many options for college upon high school graduation since his grades, at a very good school, were excellent. He considered MIT in the United States, among oth-

ers, but ultimately settled on École Polytechnique, a top engi-
neering university in Paris, at the urging of a cousin living in
France who recognized Ghosn's strength in mathematics. In
France, Ghosn was told, the best students study mathematics.
Ignoring this strength would be considered underachieving.
France was also a natural choice for Ghosn since he spoke the
language; he had been educated under a French-type system in
Lebanon and his mother was a French citizen. He did well at
the university following a slow start and later attended gradu-
ate school at École des Mines, also in Paris. During his seven
years in college he lived in the Latin Quarter of the city, an area
noted for its bohemian lifestyle, residents uniquely blending
art, intellect, and pub-crawling.

Ghosn thrived in the neighborhood, working hard and
playing hard while further expanding his global and multicultural ways of thinking and speaking. He was head of "the
American Table," a small group of French and American students who met twice a month to discuss studies, politics, and
culture. Ghosn used the informal gatherings to improve his
English, previously a textbook version learned in high school in
Lebanon.

He also toured the United States in the summer of 1976—
during the height of the bicentennial celebration—and spent
several weeks with friends in Colorado, California, and New
York, exploring new territory and improving his English. He
saw America at its best and absorbed every minute, believing
that one day he would return.

"I have a great memory of this," Ghosn says. "My image of
America was very positive, very emotional. I saw the country at
such a wonderful time and the images stayed with me."

Early Morning Call

Because he was learning at the best schools in France, Ghosn was never concerned with what he might do upon graduation. He focused instead on what might be useful to him in any profession, anywhere, like English and a broad knowledge of the world. He loved being a student and did not consider working until the suggestion came from an unsolicited, early morning telephone call.

Ghosn had been up late the night before studying and, like most of the neighborhood around him, was sound asleep when the phone rang. It was March 1978, and Carlos Ghosn, student, was about to make the transition to Carlos Ghosn, executive apprentice. The call was from a manager with the Michelin Group, the French-based, privately held company then run by Francois Michelin. The company was looking for French-educated engineers who could speak Portuguese to help with the company's entry into the Brazilian market. He had heard about Ghosn from a friend of his sister. Ghosn was completing requirements for a master's degree and contemplating getting a doctoral degree when he decided to join Michelin because the company offered him two things he wanted: a challenge and the promise of an eventual ticket back to South America.

Ghosn joined Michelin with the understanding that he would go to Brazil in the future, but first he would start at the lowest level, in a line job on a manufacturing shop floor, to learn about the company. It was the perfect place to start for a young man who would later become a leader of some of the largest manufacturing operations in the world. Ghosn saw firsthand on the shop floor the disdain factory workers can have for management, particularly those unaware of or uncaring about the daily chores and challenges of the job.

He learned a valuable lesson that he would later use as a CEO: Employees at all levels of a company have solutions to problems.

Ghosn rose through the ranks at the French tire maker quickly, managing more than 700 workers at a plant when he was just twenty-six, always under the watchful eye of the company's "managing head," Francois Michelin.

In 1984 he met Rita, the woman who would become his wife. Ghosn is an avid—make that ultracompetitive—bridge player. He and Rita met at a friend's home following a weekend bridge tournament. Rita, also from Lebanon, had just arrived in France to study pharmacology. She was ten years younger than Ghosn—still in her late teens—but mature for her age, having lived through war in Lebanon. She was also one of the rare people whose intellect and energy could keep up with Carlos Ghosn, a man already on the move.

The First Challenge

In 1985, when Ghosn was just thirty, he was named the chief operating officer of Michelin's troubled South American operations. He was told to turn the division around and to report directly to Francois Michelin. The South American operations, based in Brazil, were small by Michelin standards— $300 million in sales and 9,000 employees at two main plants—

but the challenge was large because the region was experiencing a bad case of hyperinflation.

"I had to change [employees'] salaries a couple of times per month," Ghosn says. "It was a test, but I was really eager. It was my first opportunity, and when you get that, you believe you are going to work miracles. My job was to go and fix it, no matter what."

Michelin's South American operations were suffering massive losses when Ghosn arrived, due to the runaway inflation, and nobody in management in Brazil or at company headquarters in France had an answer. He was given the job because he was the company's brightest young star. But more important, he knew Brazil.

"Some [in the company] were opposed to [me getting the job]," Ghosn says. "Francois Michelin listened to all of this and took some time before making his decision. Finally, he came to the conclusion that there were few, if any, options."

Ghosn, a newlywed, packed his bags and headed to Brazil, able to use again on a daily basis the first language he had spoken, Portuguese. All he knew about the situation in South America, really, on arrival was that inflation was out of control, so much so that diners in Brazilian restaurants, he says, often joked to waiters that they needed a check upon ordering, afraid the price would go up before their meal was completed.

What Ghosn did was look beyond the obvious, arriving to observe and listen first. Yes, inflation was a problem, but why were others so quick to give in? What Ghosn found was a company run by a multicultural mix of French and Brazilian top managers who were completely perplexed by the situation. They could not solve Michelin's problems caused by Brazil's runaway inflation because they suffered from an inability to effectively cross cultural lines and work together.

Ghosn displayed his knack for being able to look beyond the obvious, the places where others lay blame, to find the solution to company problems. He knew Brazil's inflationary problems were outside Michelin's control. The company's problems in South America started with poor internal communication and a lack of vision to past self-imposed barriers.

Ghosn believed economic conditions were just part of the problem and formed cross-cultural management teams to find the answers. It was a budding first effort at cross-cultural and cross-functional teamwork, which would later become Ghosn's signature management style. The cross-work broke barriers between the French and Brazilians and paid off for the company, making Michelin's South American division profitable within two years.

Ghosn says today Brazil "was a very intense learning experience" that showed him the importance of cross-cultural communication and experience within a company. The easy trap employees fall into is blaming internal problems on external circumstances. Different types of cross-functional teamwork remove cultural and departmental barriers, allowing solutions to be found.

Ghosn loved life in Brazil. He worked long hours, but he and Rita also enjoyed living in the country where he was born. His parents also lived there, giving them a feeling that Brazil was home.

He took a special interest in the surrounding landscape. Michelin owned two rubber plantations in the country, one in the state of Bahia and the other in the state of Matto Grasso.

Ghosn liked to walk among the trees and watch workers extracting hevea, the milky white sap that contains latex, which is made into rubber through the process known as vulcanization. One of the plantations was on flat land, manmade and very productive; the other was natural, on hilly landscape and not as productive.

The natural plantation, purchased from Firestone, had a variety of other trees on it besides the rubber trees. Michelin team members, led by Ghosn, were studying ways to increase productivity. He proposed the company set aside significant acreage for the preservation of natural species of Brazilian trees and plants. The company, with government support, planted every variety of tree native to Brazil on a reserved area of the plantation. It is known in the area as "the Ghosn garden."

Coming to America

By 1988, Ghosn's third year in Brazil with Michelin, the South American division was Michelin's most profitable in relative terms, earning him a major promotion, compliments of Francois Michelin. Ghosn, who had previously spent only a few short months in America, was named CEO of Michelin's North American operations. Carlos and Rita, now with their first child, had considered Brazil the perfect permanent home, with family members, a comfortable beach lifestyle, and competitive bridge-playing friends among the draws of Rio de Janeiro and its six million citizens. But the Ghosns moved to Greenville, South Carolina, in 1989 and began acclimating to life American style.

"When you move from Rio de Janeiro . . . lots of parties, the beach, a very fast place . . . to Greenville, South Carolina, it is quite a change," Ghosn says. "Rio is a jungle. Greenville was small, in the heart of the Bible belt. I was leaving Brazil, but gaining life in the United States."

The new position in America was the ultimate vote of confidence in Carlos Ghosn from Francois Michelin. For him to have placed the young Brazilian in charge of troubled operations in his home country was one thing; it was quite another that he gave Ghosn the latitude, trust, and opportunity to take over Michelin's North American operations when Ghosn was just in his mid-thirties. Michelin had quietly been holding discussions to acquire Uniroyal-Goodrich, a move that would double the size and headaches of Michelin North America shortly after Ghosn was to take over. A leader with cross-cultural and under-fire management experience was needed.

"That's exactly why Francois Michelin wanted Carlos Ghosn on the job," says Jim Morton, a Nissan North America senior vice president who worked at Michelin North America in Greenville with Ghosn. "He obviously saw something in Carlos Ghosn . . . he knew if anybody could handle this merger it was him."

Morton, at the time director of public relations and government affairs for Michelin North America, says Ghosn arrived in Greenville quietly with "great transparency," showing employees he had no preconceived plan and wanted input from them about what the company needed. Ghosn held numerous meetings with employees at all levels to learn about the company. "Not just management," Morton says. "He wanted to fully understand all aspects of the company from the bottom up. He was very observant and listened to everything that was said."

Ghosn arrived at Michelin North America with a lofty reputation within the company because of the work he had done turning around operations in South America. It was no secret that he was on a fast track and was getting the toughest assignments the company had to offer.

Observe and Learn from New Surroundings

Ghosn gave few, if any, immediate directives at Michelin North America. He just asked questions. It was a more fine-tuned version of his management style, which involves arriving with no preconceived notions and learning from those around him by listening.

The strategy:

- Assume nothing (find answers within the company)
- Work fast
- Earn trust and respect with strong results

He liked the business climate at Michelin North America, despite the fact that Francois Michelin and others from headquarters in France took a more active role in the much larger North American operations than they had with Ghosn in Brazil. He was enjoying, for the first time, a chance to focus on purer management principles, like consumer satisfaction and internal structure, rather than putting out the fires of Brazil's hyperinflation, constant government intervention, and high employee turnover. But the job was far from easy. His biggest challenge was maneuvering the company through its acquisition of Uniroyal-Goodrich, which, beginning in 1990, doubled the size of Michelin North America overnight in terms of employees, plants, and headaches.

Both companies made tires, but the difference in the way they operated was as contrasting as night and day. Uniroyal-Goodrich was unionized; Michelin was not. Uniroyal-Goodrich was an American company, focused primarily on short-term profits; Michelin was a privately owned French company concerned with long-term investment and product advances. The list could go on.

"The acquisition made for some interesting moments," Ghosn says.

The U.S. Department of Justice had to approve the merger, and senators and representatives on the state and national levels had plenty to say about plants that might be closed as a result. Morton, in charge of public relations and government affairs efforts for Michelin North America, never worried about what could have been his greatest liability—a new CEO who could not vote in the country and had no home field advantage politically speaking. But Ghosn tackled the lobbying aspect with a passion, using his intellect and direct, factual style to his advantage.

"[Ghosn] just loved the American political scene," Morton says. "He still talks about those days. He was such a great guy to take to Washington because all you had to do was tell him the mission. He always stayed on message and he wasn't afraid to ask [politicians] directly for what we needed . . . he knows how to get a commitment."

A Learned Lesson: Cross-Fertilization Works

The merger created for Ghosn the task of having to find ways to blend strikingly different cultures and business philosophies—the French long-term, analytical approach versus the quick, bottom-line results approach used by Americans. He relied on a technique similar to the one he had used in South America to break cultural and philosophical barriers between people: He created teams of employees from different cultures and functions within the company . . . teams of employees who would not have communicated unless directed with a strong arm. Some teams included French and Americans; others engineers and purchasing managers.

It was Ghosn's biggest effort at solving problems with cross-company and cross-functional teams. The cross-functional work allowed the French and Americans to merge and blend their management styles, taking the best each had to offer, instead of one dominating the other. The result was a successful merger and strong Michelin operations that continue in North America.

"One important lesson remains with me to this day," Ghosn said. "Neither the French nor the American management style was absolutely superior to the other. They both contributed something important and positive to the company. There was a lot of cross-fertilization of the companies and today Michelin North America is much stronger."

That he was not French or American gave him strength in orchestrating the international merger since he was not painted into one corner or the other due to cultural stereotyping. It reinforced something Ghosn had gotten small tastes of in

France and in South America: being an outsider can be used as a management advantage.

"The fact of my being not typically French and not American helped . . . people never see your decision linked to cultural shortsightedness. When you have a lot of changes to make [being an outsider] is more of an asset."

Time for a Change

Francois Michelin was proud of Ghosn's success in a personal way since he had trusted him with big assignments in Brazil and the United States. Michelin showed affection for his North American CEO when the two got together.

"You could tell that Mr. Michelin always had a special fondness for Carlos Ghosn," Morton says. "When [Francois Michelin] would come to the United States we would have company get-togethers and there were always hugs, very warm greetings, between Mr. Michelin and Carlos Ghosn . . . it went both ways."

Despite this admiration and affection, Ghosn, still in his thirties, in 1992 had climbed as far up the Michelin ladder as he could go. Three managing partners ran Michelin, and when one of these positions came open in 1992, Francois picked his son, Edouard, as the new managing partner, sending a strong message to Greenville, South Carolina.

Ghosn knew that since his last name was not Michelin, the level of advancement he stood to reach within the tightly held, family-run company was limited. Michelin was a close-knit company in which managers were rewarded and not expected to leave and Ghosn was Francois Michelin's hand-picked star.

But he is a Ghosn, not a Michelin, and he accepted the fact that he would likely not become a managing partner in the company. He realized the day would come when he would have to leave Michelin to find bigger opportunities. Ghosn worked harder than before. And a sign of how much respect Francois Michelin had for Ghosn was shown after the announcement was made that Edouard was becoming a managing partner of the company: Edouard Michelin, one of three managing heads at Michelin, was placed under Ghosn in North America. The man who had been knighted to run the company worked under and learned from the man who had proven himself on two different continents in less than ten years' time.

"It was a strange situation, Edouard being a managing partner and Carlos Ghosn being his boss," Morton says. "But they made it work. Mr. Michelin knew his son was going to be head of the company one day and he wanted him to learn from Carlos Ghosn. That just shows how much he thought of Ghosn."

Man from Mars

The Ghosns thrived in Greenville, actively participating in the community. The family grew to four children— three daughters and a son—who went to a private school in Greenville for which Ghosn served on the board of directors. The close-knit family was living the American dream via Lebanon, France, and South America: nice neighborhood, strong community, four kids, a family van, Fourth of July celebrations, and frequent visits from extended family.

When Furman University's annual music festival rolled around and food was needed for Michelin's corporate VIP tent, Rita Ghosn supervised all the cooking herself, considering it the perfect opportunity to expose others to Lebanese food. She cooked it, delivered it, and watched guests sample original, homemade international fare in an otherwise catered environment.

Michelin began a massive restructuring effort at the family-controlled company in the mid-1990s and Ghosn's new role with the company would force him to eventually move to the company's headquarters in Clermont-Ferrand, France, if he stayed. So when a headhunter from Paris called in 1996 offering Ghosn, the auto supplier, a top position with Renault, the automaker, change was imminent.

The Ghosns moved to Paris and Carlos took the job as number-two executive at Renault in October 1996, answering only to CEO Louis Schweitzer, a relative of Nobel Prize–winning physician Albert Schweitzer. Ghosn liked Schweitzer from the start, but found Renault to be a company in trouble, having suffered its first loss in ten years in 1996—$1 billion of red ink—and in the midst of becoming a listed company as the French government divested itself of majority ownership.

Schweitzer received some questioning from the media for hiring Ghosn, an outsider, to step into the number-two position at the company without the benefit of a proving period. After all, Ghosn may have been French-educated and formerly French employed, but he was the first person not born in France and the youngest to hold such a high executive post at Renault, a company for which citizens held nationalistic pride since it was controlled by the government until the year before Ghosn's arrival. And he had worked for a maker of tires, not autos.

"A newspaper headline depicted me as a Martian," Ghosn says. "I was completely foreign, coming from a supplier to work as the number-two person at an automaker . . . I was really the Martian. It was quite a bet by Louis Schweitzer."

Ghosn saw in Renault a company that was too dependent on its home market and crippled by its past failures. Renault had tried to expand outside of Europe in the 1980s when it took a large stake in American Motors, at the time makers of Jeep, but ultimately sold the line off to Chrysler at a major loss upon the realization that the company didn't have the automotive knowledge, clout, or product line to succeed in the American market. The AMC debacle was such a black eye Renault has not been back to the United States since.

Schweitzer also pursued a merger with Volvo in 1992 that proceeded to advanced stages amid high publicity in France and Sweden; but the deal ultimately failed because Renault, at the time under complete control by the French government, lacked the ownership nimbleness it needed for such a massive undertaking.

As executive vice president at Renault, Ghosn was in charge of research, purchasing, manufacturing, and engineering and car programs. He also supervised the Mercosur for Renault. But his main responsibility amid the company's heavy losses was simple: cost reduction. He analyzed every aspect of the company and determined that cuts were needed in every phase for Renault to regain credible financial strength. The result was a three-year plan to reduce operating costs by FFr20 billion in three years, a number that seemed so far-fetched at the time that some French coworkers thought Ghosn had misplaced a zero.

Ghosn's plan and methods to reduce costs included cutting from every area in the company, from administrative to engineering and manufacturing, and created a national stir. He recommended closing Renault's plant in Vilvoorde, Belgium, eliminating 3,500 jobs and creating a firestorm for Renault among European political leaders and media types, who accused the company of heartless action. Ghosn was nicknamed "le cost killer" in the media for the aggressive tactics. The point his attackers may have missed was that his plan was careful not to reduce levels of innovation at Renault and was designed to create greater long-term opportunities for jobs and growth. Tough love now produces a better child later.

Ghosn knew he was walking into a difficult situation when he accepted the job from Schweitzer. It is what he liked about the opportunity, believing once again that as somewhat of an outsider he would have an easier time implementing drastic change. Schweitzer agreed; it was one reason he took a chance on Ghosn in the first place.

"I knew it would be tough, but under difficult circumstances was the best way for me to join the Renault team," Ghosn says.

The plan worked.

By 1997 Renault was profitable again.

By 1998 Renault was strong enough that when Ghosn passed the notion to fellow executives that they consider taking a controlling stake in struggling Japanese automaker Nissan, nobody laughed.

CHAPTER THREE

Creating a Global Alliance

How did a Brazilian-born leader of Lebanese descent and French citizenship become the leader of a major Japanese corporation? The answer to the often-asked question lies at the heart of why the Renault Nissan Alliance was created in the first place.

For all parties involved, there was no other choice.

Renault, strengthened by its aggressive cost-reduction plan and a resulting surge of internal confidence, faced limited growth opportunities because European sales accounted for 85 percent of the company's total volume. More than a third of those sales occurred domestically, in France. This fact, combined with the merger of European and American automakers Daimler-Benz and Chrysler, which resulted in global giant DaimlerChrysler, led Renault executives to talk openly about expansion through acquisition.

Ghosn says it was immediately clear that limited opportunities were available for Renault. Going after a European company was pointless, considering Renault needed to grow outside of Europe, since the majority of its sales were already derived there. There was also a fear of putting Renault in a position of weakness by uniting with a bigger, stronger company. He believed Nissan was the only company that had all the attributes Renault desired and needed. He began to openly push for Nissan at a directors meeting in July 1998, telling fellow Renault executives they should consider hiring some "Japanese language instructors" and that they should all begin learning Japanese.

Ghosn knew Nissan products, having driven the Cima (or Infiniti Q45 in the United States) on a test drive while at Michelin. He had also driven the old 300ZX and liked the precision and performance of the Nissan products. In short, he knew enough about Nissan to know the company had the ability to design and build good cars and assumed the company's problems were in management, a primary strength of Renault. He also thought Nissan's top management would be less threatened by Renault and its management team since it was a company previously on a path of decline followed by a revival. The companies were similar in size and one's strength was the other's weakness.

Striking a Deal

Negotiations between the companies began in the fall of 1998, primarily in the form of talks between Schweitzer and Hanawa, Nissan's president. Nissan continued, however, holding discussions with DaimlerChrysler and also made overtures to Ford for the obvious reasons that the companies were much larger than Renault and therefore were assumed to have more clout and ability to revive the company. This caused concern among some executives at Renault and a feeling that valuable time was being wasted, since media reports hinted that larger-resource DaimlerChrysler had the upper hand in controlling Nissan. But Renault pushed on, because the risk was one worth taking since Nissan appeared to be the company's best option for growth outside of Europe. Schweitzer was determined they would give it a maximum effort until a decision was made.

Renault was better prepared for the Nissan talks as a result of experience gained from the failed merger talks with Volvo five years before. Executives impressed Nissan's Hanawa and other top executives from the start with their attention to detail and interest in letting Nissan maintain its Japanese cultural and corporate identity.

Ghosn played a limited but important role in the negotiations. When questions arose about specific ways Renault could help Nissan—outside of the $5.4 billion cash infusion—Ghosn was called in to give in-depth answers. He met with members of the Nissan executive committee for three hours, explaining in detail how Renault achieved FFr20 billion in cost reductions by forming cross-functional teams to explore problems in every area of the company.

The executive committee was impressed with Ghosn's thoroughness and the fact that he gave the entire presentation himself, something not typically done by top Japanese business executives. Ghosn prepares meticulously for such meetings, not relying on others to fill in with facts or make arguments for him. He was thorough, fact-based, and engaging, showing that he personally knew in intimate detail specific ways Nissan could save by following the example set at Renault. The meeting was a turning point for Nissan's executive committee as they realized, perhaps for the first time, that Renault was a legitimate and viable alliance candidate.

Cross-Company Teams

Negotiations continued but hit another snag when the principals took sides over the plan's details. The French were driven by "legal considerations," and tried to spell out in detail every condition and procedure the companies would follow in daily operation. The Japanese didn't like the invasive nature, preferring to proceed in a more broad-based manner. Ghosn stepped in to help, suggesting cross-company teams (CCTs) as the answer. Nissan executives liked the idea and the companies jointly formed eleven teams consisting of members from similar disciplines but different companies. The CCTs were charged with finding possible synergies between the companies and exploring specifically how these might work if an alliance was formed. Interpreters were used to facilitate communication between the French and Japanese, who were embarking on the first levels of cross-communication, which would become the cornerstone of the binational relationship.

Other large companies exploring partnerships have certainly used liaison committees and teams to study the benefits of a union or acquisition. The difference in the cross-company team format used by Renault and Nissan is that the CCTs were highly formal in function and structure and stood with the highest level of authority, despite the fact that the alliance was only under consideration.

"It was exciting from the very beginning," says Thierry Viadieu, a former Renault employee who is now a senior manager of manufacturing at Nissan. "We spent a lot of energy because [Renault team members] believed it was such a good opportunity for Nissan and Renault."

The teams studied issues in depth, using actual cases, so that both sides could see strengths and weaknesses of an alliance. Both companies opened and shared design and manufacturing files and secrets normally held only in the strictest confidence, using the translators to bridge communication gaps, which frequently showed up. An interesting element the French revealed through the CCTs' exploration process was their commitment to forming a true alliance. Renault would be forking over billions of dollars to save Nissan; but a unified, separate-but-equal tone was set by team members who worked overtime to see how varied instances of push-pull support would benefit both companies.

"It was very involved," Viadieu says, "but it had to be that way."

Convincing the Japanese that Renault was Nissan's answer was difficult since European companies don't always have strong reputations in Japan, particularly when it comes to manufacturing. Nissan might have been struggling financially with old models and overcapacity but it was a company that arguably could build a car better than any other in the world. Give us management and give us money, but please don't get in our way when it comes to building cars.

The CCTs recommended by Ghosn helped the executives and managers at both companies sort through the issue of whether Renault and Nissan could work together in a very preliminary, but concrete, way. "It was an important question. 'Do you think you can work with Renault people?' " Viadieu says. "In the beginning, they did not know the answer. We had to show them very precisely how it would work and how it would benefit Nissan."

Managers at Nissan say the manufacturing CCT case studies, done before formal creation of the alliance, contributed heavily to Nissan's quick turnaround because so much necessary legwork had already been done. Teams studied product planning, vehicle engineering, power trains, and purchasing. For example, in 2001 Renault began selling cars in Mexico that are made at a Nissan manufacturing plant in Cuernavaca, Mexico, allowing Renault to reenter a crucial market and Nissan to increase its all-important factory utilization rates. Nissan announced the Mexico manufacturing plan in December 1999, just eight months after the Renault Nissan Alliance was formed—much sooner than it would have happened had the alliance occurred without cross-company teams working in-depth beforehand. The joint manufacturing arrangement in Mexico was one of the specific projects the CCTs studied.

Such pre-alliance work served the dual purpose of showing that top managers from engineering and manufacturing could work together and of building a usable framework of synergies that could be implemented upon agreement. The bottom line: CCTs were concrete planning in action.

Some teams focused on manufacturing and logistics, while others focused on a key region like Europe or Mexico. The teams leveraged strengths of both companies, finding specific areas in which one company had needs and the other solutions. They were careful not to pursue areas that diminished market share or the corporate identity of the other, focusing instead on areas where synergy created growth and profit opportunities for both.

Renault was considering saving Nissan, but teams functioned in a cooperative spirit that would define the alliance from the start.

Signing Papers

DaimlerChrysler pulled out of negotiations on March 11, 1999, leaving Nissan no choice but to accept Renault's offer. The company was in dire straits, having been warned in February by Moody's Investment Service and Standard & Poor ratings services that its credit rating would be reduced to junk bond status within 90 days unless a cash infusion from another automaker was received. Schweitzer and Hanawa signed the Renault Nissan Alliance on March 27, 1999.

It was more than a mixing of French chardonnay and Japanese sushi. Renault would blend its management and product planning strengths with Nissan's skills in manufacturing and engineering, creating common ground for two entirely separate companies. Renault gave Nissan a $5.4 billion cash infusion in exchange for a 36.8 percent equity stake in the company. The agreement guaranteed Renault's right to increase its ownership to a maximum of 44.4 percent at a future date. Nissan also wanted to keep its corporate name, select a new COO, and maintain say-so in restructuring efforts.

These were the same terms agreed to before Daimler-Chrysler dropped its interest in acquiring Nissan. Schweitzer, in a strategic, peacekeeping move aimed at building lasting trust from Hanawa and other Nissan executives, decided against renegotiating the contract on Nissan's weakened position when Daimler-Chrysler dropped out. This careful handling of the deal was evident down to the formal wording—the Renault Nissan Alliance—which allowed both companies to maintain separate identities and avoid negatives associated with the term merger. Renault was not staging a French takeover of a Japanese company; it was lending a rather large hand and expecting the favor to be returned in the future by way of profits and growth opportunities.

The companies jointly announced that three Renault executives would be appointed to Nissan's board and make the move to Tokyo. Ghosn, executive vice president at Renault was named Nissan's chief operating officer. Patrick Pelata, senior vice president, vehicle development of Renault, would be Nissan's executive vice president of product planning and strategy. Pelata, who graduated from the same prestigious engineering university in Paris as Ghosn, is a vehicle development specialist known for his ability to streamline and maintain focus on multiple projects. Thierry Moulonguet, senior vice president, capital expenditure controller of Renault, was named managing director, deputy chief financial officer, now CFO of Nissan. Hanawa, Nissan's president, was appointed to Renault's board of directors.

Nissan got the option of taking a stake in Renault at a later date and Renault purchased Nissan's European financial operations ($320 million). The cross-company teams were formally and publicly introduced to study additional synergies that could result from the alliance in such areas as joint manufacturing and purchasing. The CCTs were essentially the same as the ones studying partnership benefits that were established at Ghosn's suggestion before, but their breadth was expanded to ensure that all possible strengths of the alliance would be explored and updated throughout the relationship between Nissan and Renault.

The alliance concept, unique in nature because it is unlike any other corporate relationships in the world, was that cross-company teams would expand their exploratory scope in increasing manners as time passed. It has nothing in common with a typical corporate acquisition or merger where ideas and mandates of one are dictated to the other, snuffing out one's culture.

The alliance, like Ghosn's views on nationality, was founded on the principle that the corporate cultures at Renault and Nissan would get additive benefits without losing identity.

On the Brink of Disaster

Of course there was no question when the alliance was signed that Nissan was the benefactor and Renault the savior. It meant relief and survival for Hanawa and Nissan. A check for $5.4 billion in cash goes a long way when debt is the enemy. For Renault, it was a moment of exhilaration laced with panic. Nissan had a good name, good products, strong manufacturing plants, and thousands of strong and seasoned employees through the highest ranks. It also had a pile of trouble, a big deal for Renault considering its small size relative to other companies previously looking at Nissan.

Ghosn, in fact, compared Renault's $5.4 billion investment at the time to a family taking its savings from the cookie jar to invest in a risky venture. The money Renault invested was all Schweitzer and company had to offer financially speaking. If Nissan continued to lose money and needed more, both companies would have problems. Renault was taking a major risk, albeit a calculated one.

"Failure was not an option," Ghosn said.

But failure was on the minds of more than a few. Debt, a staggering $22 billion, was a secret to none. Nor was the fact that Nissan, which once sold one-third of all vehicles in Japan and dominated North America from a foreign automaker's perspective, attaining status as 1975's No. 1 import, was in a decades-long slump, sales in Japan on a declining trend for more than a quarter century.

The facts: Nissan's domestic market share, which peaked at 34 percent in 1974, declined to below 19 percent in 1999. Nissan's global market share declined from 6.6 percent in 1991 to 4.9 percent in 1999, an eight-year period in which the company had just one profitable year.

The surprise: how deeply Nissan was plagued by a deep, imbedded sense of resignation and helplessness held by executives and managers, conditioned by years of backpedaling, failed resuscitation efforts, a hurting Japanese economy, and debilitating cultural business traditions.

The tendency at Nissan was to blame the company's ill fate on everything that seemed to be logically responsible, ignoring the fact that chief competitors Honda and Toyota experienced growth and profits during the 1990s. The bursting of Japan's economic bubble, which fueled the country's postwar surge, got most of the blame. Companies like Nissan, having expanded rapidly overseas in the 1980s, were faced with large debts they couldn't pay when the bubble burst. Japanese companies found restructuring difficult. They were caught in the middle of a cultural squeeze play, needing to cut costs on one side and having a responsibility to employees and corporate traditions on the other.

At Japan Inc., jobs are for life. It may be nothing for Western corporations to axe 3,000 jobs at a single press conference. In Japan, such measures are taboo. You take a job, work hard for years at lower levels, then rise through the ranks to bigger paychecks, more perks, and less work. Leaving one company after years on the job to work at another is accepting the previously nonflattering professional title in Japan of a "midcareer" hire. When companies struggle, changes are discussed, but layoffs and plant closings rarely occur, preserving jobs for employees until they are ready to leave or retire. Nissan launched several revival-type plans during the 1990s before Ghosn arrived but none ever stuck because the political environment eroded management's confidence in the plans.

Nissan, under the leadership of Yoshifumi Tsuji (1992–1996), announced in 1993 a plan designed to return Nissan to profitability by 1997. The company even closed a plant, the first such move in Japan's automotive industry since 1945. But intervention from management and labor unions softened the blow, workers gradually transferred to other plants in the country, and the plan fizzled from there.

"Management just wanted to exist and move along, not cause trouble," says Emil Hassan, a Nissan North America senior vice president and a veteran of the company for more than twenty years. "Management believed 'these problems, they will fix themselves, if we just give them time.' "

Hassan, named in 2001 to the *Automotive News* "Dream Team" as the world's leading manufacturing executive, was one of several Americans at the company who suggested through the years specific ways Nissan could reduce operating expenses and improve profitability only to be shot down. Nissan had developed a loyal following in the United States. Nissan North America, with its headquarters in the Los Angeles area, design and engineering facilities in San Diego and Detroit (Farmington Hills), and a manufacturing facility in Tennessee, was developing, building, and selling cars at a profit better than Nissan was in Japan. But NNA operations were almost autonomous and the Japanese showed very little interest in taking advice from U.S. executives when it came to how-to. They met and talked, but that was it.

"We tried so many times to do differently," Hassan says. "We talked about it, but little was ever done."

The company was so confused during what North American employees often refer to as the "dark ages" of the 1990s that a million dollars was spent and a grand, public party thrown for the last Z car when the model was taken off the U.S. market. That Nissan was spending money to promote a car it could no longer sell during tough financial times sounds ludicrous now but was typical of the times. The company faced manufacturing capacity in Japan so high the company could produce a million more vehicles than it could possibly sell.

Nissan was also paying suppliers 15 to 20 percent more than other automakers for goods. And its brand power (consumer belief of a product's worth) had eroded to the point that

Ghosn quickly learned that Nissan essentially gave away more than $1,000 for every car it sold in the United States in comparison with Japanese competitor Toyota, a result of marketing dollars cut during hard times and no cohesive global strategy.

Nissan slowed investment in its aging product line, letting models like the March in Japan (or Micra in Europe) fall several years behind those of competitors, despite once holding an edge. The March won the 1992 and 1993 Japanese Car of the Year award and the Micra was Car of the Year in Europe in 1993 but the model was completely outdated by 1999 and sales were sagging. Other cost reduction experimentations came in the way of cheaper toilet paper and raised thermostats in company facilities—anything to buy more time and avoid having to face the company's real problem: unwillingness to challenge Japanese business traditions.

"Nissan used to have a management structure that worked . . . because the economy was good," says Akira Sato, vice president of treasury and a twenty-five-year veteran at Nissan. "But when the bubble burst, this same style did not work. We were struggling, and nobody had the answer."

Trapped by Tradition

Keiretsu, or business groups linked by shared values, business ties, and cross shareholdings, formed in Japan after World War II when the United States forced the breakup of several large industrial groups, called zaibatsus, that had dominated economic activity through central ownership and control. The zaibatsus were dissolved, but a number of others quickly sprouted up, evolving into keiretsu. Typically these keiretsu coalesced around a bank or large manufacturer. The major characteristic of the keiretsu is the cross-holding of stock, a ploy that prevents takeover threats from foreign corporations and reduces pressure on management to achieve short-term results.

Large keiretsu keep many exports out of the country because members purchase goods and services from each other, supporting the domestic network. Keiretsu benefited Japanese companies, particularly automakers, during periods of economic growth because the supply chain was so closely linked to manufacturing needs, providing solutions and products quickly. Keiretsu, typically made up of noncompetitors, can also cover losses in the network of a weak link, and struggling companies often send workers to more prosperous industries in the network. This helping-others-at-all-costs attitude often runs so deeply through a keiretsu that the bank at the group's core extends debt payments and even lends more money to struggling companies.

Nissan was overinvested in and beholden to companies that had little to do with its primary automotive business, holding ownership in 1,394 different companies before they formed the Renault alliance. Nissan went so far as to own 50 percent of its own car dealerships in Japan, essentially killing entrepreneurial sales incentives domestically. Nissan's supply costs, due to its keiretsu relationships, reached levels the company could no longer operate profitably because many senior managers of suppliers were former Nissan employees. Heads of the keiretsu companies also often hold close social ties, enjoying lavish expense accounts and private club memberships, creating more pressure to maintain the long-standing relationships. It was no different at Nissan, a company the Japanese considered conservative and traditional even before the Renault alliance, making it difficult for the company to buy outside the group despite better prices.

"They just refused to see reality," a veteran Nissan manager says. "Everybody knew there was a problem, and they all had part of the solution, but couldn't put the puzzle together."

Still, Hanawa tried, as his predecessor had. He announced the Global Business Reform Plan in 1998. But by 1999 the company had 148,000 employees and layers of executives without a cause. In December 1998 Nissan had to borrow $708 million in emergency funds from state-owned Japan Development Bank just to stay afloat. Global divisions complicated Nissan's structure. Nissan North America and Nissan Europe were run like separate entities when it came to finances, sales, and marketing. This weakened Nissan's global brand identity and its efforts to create real change.

"When [senior managers] would come [to the United States]," a former Nissan North America employee says, "it was more like a vacation . . . an hour or two of meetings with a tee time and a dinner reservation. [Nissan North America] was the strongest unit they had. Suggestions were given [on how to fix the company]. They would listen, and they would make plans, but nothing was ever really done."

Nissan sold 2.4 million automobile units worldwide in 1999, a decline of almost 300,000 from 1996, the last year before the alliance that it posted a profit. Sales in the United States slumped in 1997 and 1998 due to the dated and limited product lines, but the biggest difference was in Japan, where sales in

1996 totaled 1.1 million units versus 758,000 in 1999. Nissan's 1996 profit was small, just 78 billion yen earned in net income from 6.6 trillion yen in net sales, but significantly better than the 684 billion yen Nissan lost in 1999, which was the company's largest net deficit ever.

Strength in America

The company certainly had strengths before the Renault alliance, particularly in the United States. Models like Xterra, the sport-utility vehicle made at Nissan's Smyrna, Tennessee, plant and the Maxima, a mid-size sedan, experienced loyal, and in some cases, rabid, followings. Xterra, launched in 1999, was on its way to becoming a Generation X "must have" before Ghosn and company arrived, winning North American Truck of the Year its first year. The SUV is honored by Xterra fan clubs and websites and is often the most visible vehicle on college campuses around the country. Nissan produces roughly 85,000 Xterras in Smyrna annually. The Maxima has for years experienced similar success, drawing buyers back again and again.

The Maxima and Xterra, as well as the popular Pathfinder, came out of Nissan Design America (NDA), the company's North American design center in San Diego now under the direction of Tom Semple. Known for years as Nissan Design International, the center developed U.S.-specific vehicle plans, receiving ultimate approval from Japan.

Manufacturing was strong in America as well. The

Harbour Report North America 2002 named Nissan as the most efficient manufacturing nameplate in North America for the eighth consecutive year, evidence of Nissan's heritage of manufacturing productivity dating back before the first whisper of an alliance with Renault. The Smyrna plant, under the leadership of Hassan and Dan Gaudette (senior vice president, U.S. manufacturing), produces three models: the Altima sedan, Xterra SUV, and a full line of Frontier trucks. (Production of the Maxima will start in early 2003.) The same can be said for design and administration in North America. They were pockets of strength disjointed and disconnected from benefits that come from global brand cohesion.

The Blame Game

Practically all of Nissan's strengths, whether in product or personnel, were isolated from one another. A little good here and there means nothing to a company with 140,000 employees and operations spread across the world. Cross-communication was almost nonexistent at Nissan, as was professionalism and savvy in key areas like product planning and marketing on a global basis. This created a severe case of corporate separation, and, as a result, finger-pointing.

A culture of blame developed within the company, particularly in Japan. If the company did poorly, it was always someone else's fault, Ghosn says. Departments blamed each other and regional operations blamed each other. Sales blamed product planning; product planning blamed engineering. Tokyo blamed Europe, and Europe blamed Tokyo. It was a never-ending cycle of buck-passing frustration that left Nissan in a years-long slump.

That is why critics were not convinced in 1999 that Ghosn and fellow Renault gaijin, or foreigners, could save Nissan. There was general agreement over the diagnosis of the company—that it had been going through the motions, making outdated cars just to keep people in jobs; but how—if—it could be fixed was up for debate. Knowing the problems is one thing, repairing them another. Some journalists openly doubted whether Ghosn and the team from Renault could turn Nissan around in several years, if at all, citing market factors around the world that went far beyond the company's internal problems.

Ghosn says he never doubted the significance of the challenges he faced in his new job, but spent no time considering "what ifs," knowing that if Nissan was not completely and thoroughly revived, the blame this time would fall directly on him.

CHAPTER FOUR

Always Start with a Clean Sheet of Paper

When Carlos Ghosn arrived in Tokyo in the spring of 1999 to serve as Nissan's chief operating officer, his baggage included a handful of nicknames and a reputation in some corners as a Western-business hatchet man.

Ghosn was not the first foreigner to lead a Japanese automaker. An American had led Mazda for a couple of years beginning in 1996 when Ford Motor Company took a controlling stake in it. But Ghosn's arrival drew more attention in Japan and around the world because expectations were that he would make drastic moves, considering his "cost killer" reputation and Nissan's poor health. The first day Ghosn showed up for work at Nissan's Tokyo headquarters, everyone, from Japanese media to entry-level Nissan employees, knew he was a harbinger of change for Japan Inc. and the automaker. The questions were only, How many and How fast?

Yet Ghosn, with no time to spare given Nissan's ailing disposition, did not arrive in Japan with an A to Z blueprint to rescue the company. Instead, he looked carefully for answers from within before rushing to judgment. This was the same technique he had used at Michelin and Renault. It had proven so successful that he carried it steps farther this time, seeking more input from more employees at all levels of the company.

No Prefabricated Solutions

Ghosn strongly believes that when assessing new people, places, and challenges, it is imperative to cleanse the mind of any preconceived notions and ideas. It's a primary assessment tool he uses to avoid being influenced by stereotypes of a culture, company, or both, before first observing realities firsthand.

Always Start with a Clean Sheet of Paper

"This is extremely important in management," Ghosn says. "You must start with a clean sheet of paper because the worst thing you can have is prefabricated solutions . . . you have to start with a zero base of thinking, cleaning everything out of your mind."

Ghosn said he had a very vague, but positive, image of Japan, before his arrival, but he erased even this upon arrival to start anew. "You have to have the approach of a scientist. [A scientist] has a lot of knowledge, but his knowledge is only a tool. Observation of fact brings him the solution."

Ghosn spent his early days and months on the job traveling throughout Nissan's worldwide network, making stops at automotive design centers and manufacturing plants in Japan, Europe, and North America.

The idea is that during the first weeks and months a new leader is on the job, others at the company typically sit, wait, wonder, and speculate before jumping to conclusions. By getting in the field quickly and meeting people, you learn the company and its people firsthand, while getting the added benefit of "shortening the distance" with others who have preconceived notions about you—"le cost killer."

Ghosn would fly for a dozen hours or more from Tokyo to Nissan locations for his visits but get off the plane fresh and ready to go—working, meeting, and absorbing information from others for hours. He shook hands with and greeted employees at all levels, holding engaging and personal minibrainstorming sessions with executives and line workers. At the end of the day, usually when flying to another location, he would recall to colleagues the most minute and specific details from what he had heard, having already processed information from hours of meetings and handshaking. He used this information to chart and plot a picture of Nissan from a worldwide perspective, identifying the problems that created a disjointed, unprofitable, lagging brand.

"His energy was amazing," says Debra Sanchez Fair, Nissan North America vice president of corporate communications. "He got off the airplane ready to work and would go all day long, absorbing it all."

Nissan employees saw Ghosn as a personable man with diverse knowledge and a focus on saving the company and empowering the people to run it. His personality, a sort of global familiarity, makes others comfortable despite his always-present intensity and fast-moving style, showing Nissan's people the hatchet-man was human after all.

One of Ghosn's first visits was to Smyrna to see the company's award-winning manufacturing plant. What he found was a man in charge who had grown weary after years of fighting political battles with management in Tokyo. Emil Hassan, a senior vice president at Nissan North America, was a company veteran of more than twenty years who was ready for a new challenge—at another company.

Hassan told Ghosn about problems that had plagued the company and solutions that had been offered in the past but had fallen victim to corporate apathy. Ghosn listened. Then, he responded with intensity and a commitment to create change—quickly. He talked with a focus and clarity that showed Hassan a new day was dawning at Nissan.

"After our first meeting I went home and told my wife, 'There is something different about this man,'" Hassan says. "It had gotten to the point that I just did not think I had the energy to keep talking about change but never doing anything about it for ten years. When I met Ghosn . . . it's hard to describe. The charisma and confidence was obvious. I thought, This man is exactly what Nissan needs. I knew we would get the job done."

Ghosn is like an analytical, conversational computer in meetings. He processes information and thoughts so fast that others are amazed at his rapid conceptualization, the way he sifts through facts and puts his fingers directly on problems. During his initial fact-finding tour, that meant quickly identifying the points that were crippling the automaker. He met with others, probed with comfortable candor, and listened. Then, he would make a direct strike, exposing the uncovered issue he is looking for. His intensity level rises while he looks for obvious solutions, refusing to let the problem lie dormant. When solutions are not obvious, plans are put in place to rapidly find them through whatever means are necessary.

Hassan remembers going with Ghosn and Pelata to the Nissan Technical Center North America in Michigan, just outside of Detroit. The center is the heart of product research, development, and engineering for Nissan North America. A senior manager was explaining why more expensive parts were used on a specific vehicle when he and others at NTC wanted to use less expensive parts that provided the same consumer benefit.

"Why?" Ghosn asked the manager, demanding a logical answer.

"Because I don't have the authority [to do differently]," the manager responded.

Ghosn: "You believe the other is better and less expensive?"

Manager: "But I do not have the authority."

Ghosn was incensed. Communication was so poor within the company that senior managers had little or no authority to improve the company when they knew what needed to be done.

A directive was given, on the spot.

"I give you authority," Ghosn said. "Now, you have the authority."

This type of problem had existed for years—Americans resigned to thinking they could not change Japanese management styles and habits. Many simply gave up over time, saying it couldn't be done. Here came Ghosn, touring with blinders on about the past and thinking quickly on his feet about the future.

You *can* do it. I am *telling* you to do it. *Now*, you have the authority.

Nissan was changing already.

"Seeing, brainstorming, getting in the field and gathering as much information as possible . . . deeply listening," Ghosn says. "I talked to people at all levels, at the plant level, at the management level, on the shop floor. There is a lot you can learn and understand by talking to the people and listening to what they have to say."

What Ghosn learned about individuals was that they had lost confidence in the company and the country and to a large degree questioned whether anything could truly be done to change the state of declining affairs. What he learned about the company as a whole during this handshaking, frank-talking period was that it suffered from a case of deep corporate depression, causing little to actually get done in the way of implementation needed to create change.

"When you go to a country that is not your own, you have to be prepared to live and adapt to that country," Ghosn says. "It should be an enjoyable experience and a learning one. I came to Japan with a lot of interests, a strong will to learn, and with a lot of respect for the country and its people. I did not come with a preconceived plan."

• • •

When not in the field, Ghosn spent time in Tokyo meeting with Nissan's Japanese workforce to learn about the company's past and glean snippets of vision for the future. His direct style, surprisingly, was not a turn-off to the Japanese, who normally function indirectly when it comes to interpersonal business relations. Ghosn was so anxious to find the problems and eager to fix the company that up close and personal was welcome from employees who realized drastic changes needed to be made.

Ghosn showed he was adaptable to his new environment and comfortable in it. He knew eyes in Tokyo would be upon him, the aggressive foreigner riding in for the rescue, so he was visible and active within the Japanese community, attending company baseball games, learning to properly eat with chopsticks (a former Nissan executive gave him an informal lesson), and attempting to learn the language.

His personal approach to the cultural challenge was no different than the course he was charting for Nissan and the alliance. He wanted to learn from and adapt to his new environment, while maintaining personal identity, a good lesson for anyone working in an international environment. If you do not adapt, you lose. If your identity is compromised, you lose.

The capacity to adapt without losing identity will be increasingly important for businesses and individuals in the twenty-first century.

Ghosn's ability to adapt to the country and the people while maintaining his sense of urgency and commitment to reform gave Nissan employees and Japanese citizens a picture of a corporate leader enjoying his new environment. "I did not have to tell [Japanese] that I like their country . . . they could see it," he says.

And he could see why Nissan was struggling, having put

together the puzzle with the pieces he gathered from employees all over the world. There were five major reasons, according to Ghosn:

- lack of a clear profit orientation
- insufficient focus on customers and too much focus on chasing competitors
- lack of cross-functional, cross-border, and intra-hierarchical lines of work in the company
- lack of a sense of urgency
- no shared vision or common long-term plan

Nissan was a company trapped by tradition and many people inside who did not believe an outsider could create necessary change. The previous failed attempts at revival left doubters no reason to think Ghosn could get all the pieces together fast enough to turn the company around before it sank further amid confusion caused by foreign leadership.

Nissan had worldwide operations, but it could hardly be called a global company in 1999. To truly be global, there must be active and working connections between the core and its regions. Nissan more closely resembled a large regional company that had ownership in other companies around the world than a unified, one-world automaker. Nissan North America had its leadership and its own set of rules; same for Nissan Europe. The problem was that ultimate control was held in Japan, where companies operate under certain time-tested practices intended to provide close-knit support and security in a tightly held, domestic fashion. The web running in Japan from keiretsu partners, including banks and other large manufacturers, to government officials to thousands of Nissan employees, was spun from a belief that change would break the ties that bind, exposing people and entities in uncommon and uncomfortable ways.

Ghosn thought Nissan needed to give those who felt threatened, who were clinging for cover under the traditions of Japan Inc., a reason to believe this turnaround effort was different from the others before and that change would be good for the company and consequently the country. Nissan was in a financial crisis and had a limited and outdated product line in 1999, and yet business was being conducted as usual every day before the alliance. The people had fallen into a trap in which it was easier to do nothing than get excited about false promises. Ghosn recognized this and worked hard to show Nissan employees that tomorrow would be too late for action.

"For so many years, changes needed to be made, but no one made them," he says. "That's why my first task was to instill a sense of urgency."

According to Ghosn, Nissan's strengths were:

- a significant international presence and global reach
- a world-leading manufacturing system
- a leading edge in selective, crucial technological fields
- the alliance with Renault
- talented and dedicated employees

Gaining Control

When the Renault Nissan Alliance was signed and made public, Renault executives were hit hard with pitches from consultants from around the world wanting to help them understand how to work within a Japanese corporation and how to handle the cultural traditions and difficulties that come with the territory. They resisted, however, believing that consultants would only slow them down and cost too much.

"Consultants were all trying to tell us how they knew better than us how to do business in Japan," says Dominique Thormann, vice president of global communications and investor relations at Nissan. He formerly worked at Renault, moving to Tokyo when the alliance was signed. "Nissan wasn't going to live too long if we didn't do something. What made working without consultants realistic is, we come to Japan knowing nothing. Carlos Ghosn doesn't believe in cultural clashes. He came here and saw Nissan only as a maker of cars and went to work from there. . . ."

The small management team that initially came to Nissan from Renault, including Pelata, Moulonguet, Thormann, and Vice President Philippe Klein, among others, worked in a very tight, top-level inner circle built around Ghosn, who as COO was officially Nissan's number-two man—Hanawa maintained his position as president in 1999—but who was clearly in charge.

"There was never a question of who made the decisions," one insider says. "[Hanawa] didn't mind. He seemed relieved."

One of the biggest challenges the management team faced from the start was gaining control of the company's communications, external and internal. Nissan had treated external communications as more of a reactionary tool than anything, sticking close to Japanese corporate tradition of telling as little as possible to the general and investment public. It was the old "no news is good news" philosophy. By doing so, the company had created a field of distrust among Japanese media through its unreliable public relations efforts during its years of struggle. There were also leaks within Nissan as managers and executives talked with media, delivering speculative messages of imminent change the "cost killer" would deliver.

Internal communications weren't much better. In Japan, Nissan's only hint of this function was found inside the human resource department, of all places. This wasn't the case at Nissan North America, where solid communication, both external and internal, were pursued, Western-style. But the isolated efforts did Nissan little good considering the majority of its 140,000-plus employees worked in Japan.

"[In Japan] we had no computer in the investor relations department," Thormann says. "We brought a computer from Renault . . . there was no communications infrastructure whatsoever."

It did not stay that way for long. Ghosn recognizes the benefits of communications like perhaps no other business leader in the world and wasted no time in building a Tokyo-based department that facilitated a proactive approach with the media and employees. He uses communications as a primary management tool to such a high degree that he often gets involved in small details of presentations and press releases, doctoring words and inserting facts.

During his first months at Nissan Ghosn carried this practice to the extreme, desperately needing to control the flow of information inside the company and out. He knew how important it was that the company gain control of information so he was "totally involved" in every communications piece. One word sending the wrong message, particularly inside the company, could derail all efforts. Ghosn knew what messages he wanted communicated and micromanaged the flow of information.

Still, Nissan's new management team met hostility from some Japanese media types who had grown weary from years of being fed blocks of raw numbers accompanied by vague answers. They also wanted immediate answers to questions about change they knew was imminent since the "cost killer" was now in charge. They were preying on any managers and executives they could get to speak out of line. "Nissan had a very antagonistic relationship with journalists at home when we got here," Thormann says. "It was ugly . . . very disjointed and disconnected. We had to close down for a while and not take any interviews."

Distributed information was released only after direct approval from Ghosn, who knew that every word, stated or printed, that came from Nissan would be heavily scrutinized while the company's reform plan was built. Ghosn personally approved everything, aides say, down to individual slides used for presentations. He believed precise and effective communication was vital during uncertain, speculative times. "He would even get involved in how a presentation slide for a meeting looked, analyzing whether lines one way or another made it confusing," one aide says. "He was incredible."

Internally, Ghosn's travels throughout Nissan's Japanese infrastructure and its global outposts made an immediate impact as employees began to believe the input they were giving him could actually play a role in saving the troubled company. His international flair and thirst for local knowledge allowed him to find common ground with people regardless of whether it was a line worker in Smyrna, Tennessee, or an executive at Nissan Europe.

Many were surprised at Ghosn's nonthreatening aura and had a feeling of familiarity with their new globetrotting leader, who showed he was comfortable in Los Angeles, Smyrna, Tokyo, and Detroit. One Nissan North America employee recalls meeting Ghosn during his fact-finding mission and says the man from France via the United States, Brazil, and Lebanon acted nothing like a man who arrived with a bigger-than-business reputation from his cost-cutting work at Renault. Employees in Japan say the same thing. They met him and he seemed "so familiar" because of his nonstereotypical posture and cultural adaptability. Word of these first internal impressions began to spread from the bowels of the company into the general public, giving Ghosn's "clean sheet of paper" approach the double effect of erasing preconceived notions about him and his style while he learned about the company he intended to save.

"I came to Japan with a big, bad wolf image," Ghosn says. "Little by little, [the Japanese people] found I was not as wolfy as they thought I was. They were saying things when I got here like, I didn't care about people. I benefited some from this big bad wolf caricature because I started as the wolf; then I was the good guy. To me, it was leverage."

Empowering the People

Although Ghosn learned a lot about Nissan and its problems—he says among the biggest realizations was the regionalization of the company and its lack of a central strategy—from the people he met with in his first weeks on the job, he knew that to succeed at a high level the plan to repair the company must come in part directly from the people within or it would fail just like previous reform efforts.

Any leader can dictate.

And he did so when needed in the beginning, like telling the NTC manager he had authority to buy the parts he believed were needed before sending the change through corporate channels. But he also believed that many of the answers needed could be found within from the people who knew the company intimately from years of experience.

The challenge was that Nissan needed to change, fast. And new ways were needed because the old ones were not working. But Ghosn could not afford to lose the trust of the Japanese people who had built the company and supported it through generations of car buying by acting in too forceful a manner. He wanted to preserve the best the culture had to offer within the company, unleashing the talent and ideas he knew were there through motivation, cultivation, and confidence.

"I was non-Nissan, non-Japanese," Ghosn says. "I knew that if I tried to dictate changes from above, the effort would backfire, undermining morale and productivity. But if I was too passive, the company would simply continue its downward spiral."

The solution: cross-functional teams (CFTs), Ghosn's patented management tactic used to revitalize the spirit of a company from the inside out.

Ghosn came to Nissan with the reputation of a corporate turnaround artist, so the fact that he was asking for solutions from inside the ailing company caught some outside the company off guard. The man with the "cost killer" reputation arrives and everyone is waiting for action. He is expected to show up, give some directives, and immediately orchestrate change with top-down orders. Ghosn did want change—immediate change—but his idea of how it would occur was different than conventional opinion. He believed that the employees inside Nissan had solutions to the problems of the company. And he had a way of finding them with his cross-functional team approach.

The CFTs were formed, consisting mostly of middle managers in the company, and told to identify problems and make recommendations to Ghosn and to Nissan's executive committee as to how they could be fixed. The CFT concept allows employees from different disciplines to work together in a structured way to solve problems. It is different than committee or operational communications meetings held at other companies because the teams at Nissan are organized and empowered at the highest levels of the company and given large-scale, but specific, tasks.

"Outside, people said, 'You can't do that,' " Ghosn says. "It's true you do have to have your own opinions and beliefs to manage in a crisis. But in corporate turnarounds, particularly one like this where you have two companies relatively the same size with different backgrounds, you have to protect the company's identity and the self-esteem of the people."

Within five days of officially starting work at Nissan, Ghosn made the decision to form nine cross-functional teams, consisting of approximately ten members each. They were drawn from Nissan's middle managers corps, a group of employees with specific line responsibilities. He challenged them as CFT members to think freely and creatively to find ways to fix Nissan, immediately.

The cross-functional teams were established according to one strong belief: The solutions to Nissan's problems were inside the company.

Ghosn uses a variety of management techniques to motivate people, solve problems, and create change, but perhaps none stands out more than his creative use of CFTs, his management signature. He first experimented with CFTs at Michelin South America in Brazil, officially utilizing them to greater degrees and larger scopes at Michelin North America and Renault before creating the model in use at Nissan today, which has been the subject of discussions in prestigious business schools such as Harvard and Stanford. CFT meetings are nothing like the Monday morning quarterback meetings at other corporations where ideas are tossed around. Teams have no direct decision-making power but they operate with authority just below the executive committee, which decides which CFT recommendations to follow.

"Formally the first time to use CFTs was in 1993 [at Michelin North America], the second time was at Renault in 1996," Ghosn says. "The most elaborate version is still being fine-tuned . . . it's a many-wave enhancement now in its third redesign."

The CFT concept is to force company employees to reach across boundaries, debating concepts and sharing information with people and departments they would typically not come into contact with in daily operations. Ghosn says it's normal that marketing people like to work only with marketing people and designers like to work only with designers—Americans are more comfortable working with Americans—but companies suffer when executives, managers, and other employees remain in functional and regional boxes.

Nissan's CFT format involves selecting managers from different disciplines and operational regions, including North America, Europe, and general overseas markets, breaking functional and cultural barriers.

"In my experience, employees in a company rarely reach across cultures and boundaries," Ghosn says. "At a global company like Nissan this is very important because employees may be from different cultures but they work for the same goals, the same company. Not only do CFTs reach across cultures . . . they allow an executive vice president to work directly with a general manager and so on."

CFTs were a strange brew at Nissan at first, considering Japanese tradition is that executives meet with executives, rarely problem-solving with workers at lower levels. Add in factors like the language barriers that existed between employees in Japan, Europe, and North America and French newcomers from Renault and the vast philosophical differences in car building between Nissan and Renault and one can see the potential that existed for corporate combustion.

"In the beginning we had two companies with very different structures and cultures," says Bernard Long, a former Renault executive now serving as vice president of international human resources at Nissan. "Renault was more concerned with product planning and policy. In the case of Nissan, this was not true. Nissan was very strongly focused on engineering. When you put the two together and add in the cocktail of people from different regions—with two citizenships—it is not an obvious thing to make work."

Ghosn's primary goal in forming the CFTs was to find ways to fix the company. But he also knew that the crash course would develop interpersonal relations between people from different background and countries faster and more effectively than any other management tool he could use.

The nine CFTs were assigned specific focus areas: business development, purchasing, manufacturing and logistics, research and development, sales and marketing, general and administrative, finance and cost, phase-out of products and parts complexity management, and organization. The teams were structured so that each had two leaders, typically executive vice presidents and members of Nissan's decision-making executive committee, and one pilot, a senior manager chosen from the ranks of the ten line managers who made up the team.

Limiting the teams to ten members provided enough employees to give varied input while keeping them small enough to allow discussions to move forward at a rapid pace. Team CFT leaders, the executive vice presidents, played somewhat removed roles in the process—they did not attend all the meetings—so that the exercises were not an extension of Nissan's old blame game. The executives acted mostly as official sounding boards for the teams. Ghosn also appointed two leaders to each CFT so that a single function, like purchasing or research and development, could not dominate.

CFT pilots, from the management ranks, were chosen with input from Ghosn so he could witness "the next generation of Nissan leaders." Pilots play the most crucial role in the CFT concept, driving the agenda and discussions of all meetings, and strong leaders are needed to keep the focus on finding solutions rather than placing blame or posturing for selfish reasons.

Each CFT had the authority to form additional team subsets, based on the reality that ten members would not have the time or resources to expose each pertinent subject if it was covered with any depth. Subteams were also composed of ten members typically. In all, more than 500 Nissan employees—the vast majority from middle management—directly participated in the initial CFTs and subteams.

The specific charge from Ghosn to the nine newly formed CFTs was to review Nissan's operations and come up with specific recommendations on how to restore profitability and future growth.

The deadline was three months.

"No sacred cows, no taboos, no constraints," he said.

The CFTs were structured so that members had no outlets to vent complaints only; they had to find solutions. Team members were granted access to all pertinent information within the company they needed but told to make sure time was spent identifying and finding answers to problems at hand.

Nissan Cross-Functional Teams Overview

CFT COMPOSITION

- **Leaders**

  Two leaders are selected from top executive ranks representing different disciplines with common ground (example: purchasing and engineering). Leaders act mainly as sounding boards and executive informational sources for each team.

- **Pilots**

  Hand-chosen by top management, pilots are responsible for keeping each team on task through agenda, research, and dialogue.

- **Members**

  Middle managers (typically nine) are selected on criteria based on areas of focus and leadership qualities.

- **Subteams**

  Composed of CFT team members and other company managers selected by the CFT team, subteams are charged with exposing specific issues with more depth.

CFT GUIDELINES

- Nothing is off limits to discuss and explore. Teams are not to be hindered by traditions or avoid sensitive corporate issues. Teams can also look into any aspect of company operations. Teams should come up with ambitious yet realistic ideas.

- Teams have no decision-making power; they can only make recommendations to the executive committee.

Telling Japanese managers they had no barriers when it came to recommendations they could make to the executive committee was a gift rarely given to middle ranks in Japan. The unfamiliar territory caused teams to start slow. Leaders and pilots—all Japanese—were unsure of themselves and the charge they had been given, creating some anxious moments among the former Renault executives, who wondered if they understood the urgency Ghosn had worked to instill.

But teams began moving faster once members saw they had truly been given a no-strings proposition and empowerment to find ways to fix the company. Brainstorming took off and ideas flowed once team members got to know each other and broke the barriers that previously had existed.

Working on a Fast Track

Ghosn's reason for giving the CFTs so little time to reach conclusions about exact measures that needed to be taken to rescue the company was simple. Renault was so heavily invested it could not afford to be dragged down by Nissan for long, and it was immediately apparent to Ghosn and others that the company's short-term prospects were not good without a new plan to implement. Also, speculation both inside and outside the company as to what the Renault team would recommend in terms of change was so intense that every passing day spent without a public plan to turn the company around added more anxiety in Japan to an already stressful situation.

Ghosn gave each team broad issues to study, with the

expectation that they would provide specific responses. For instance, the business development CFT, represented by managers from product planning, engineering, manufacturing, and sales and marketing, was charged with focusing its review on profitable growth, new product opportunities, brand identity, and product development lead time. In other words, this one CFT had to determine what type of new products Nissan needed; which new products would be the most profitable; how these new products fit the company's global brand identity; how Nissan's global brand identity could be strengthened—all in a short span of three months, or less when you factor in the necessary personal acquaintanceship period.

Nissan in 1999 was a company that had been in business for more than sixty-five years with a poor financial condition resulting from a decade or more of bad decisions and inadequate leadership. The thought that nine teams and dozens of other subsets could study, research, and find ways to completely revitalize the company in just three months was incomprehensible to some, including key team members not used to working on something so drastic, so rapidly.

Some complained.

Some said more time was needed.

Some said it could not be done at all.

No Time to Waste

But Carlos Ghosn is not a patient man. His patience, or lack thereof, can be a weakness. But in this instance, the man who hates lines and can't wait for storytellers to get to the punch line, made his impatience work to his advantage, telling CFTs there was no choice—no choice—but to focus on assigned tasks and deliver corporate objectives in three months' time. The message was simple and clear: Get to work and get it done.

"I arrived in Tokyo on a Friday and was working on the revival plan by Monday morning," says Viadieu, the only Renault expatriate to work in manufacturing in Tokyo. "Mr. Ghosn said, 'We have no time.'"

Ghosn had originally wanted CFT objectives to be reached in two months, but granted a third month, realizing that more time was needed to reach the depths of reform he desired. Managers say they worked harder than ever before during their time as CFT pilots and members, many surrendering traditional Japanese summer vacations and giving up other work responsibilities to get the job done.

Progress was slow in the beginning since the cross-functional method—engineers working with managers from finance and purchasing—was so new to mostly Japanese team members. Nissan is a big company where before CFTs segregation occurred by segmentation. Middle-level engineers and middle-level purchasing managers might not have ever come into contact with one another despite the fact that they were supposedly working for common goals.

"Frankly speaking, we had some anxious moments in the beginning," says Long, referring to Nissan's new French ex-pats. "These were teams built with people from different regions, different functions . . . many out of hierarchical line. For the first month, our impression was that nothing was moving."

The French executives were right. CFT pilots paint a kind

of deer-in-headlights scenario when reflecting upon the first weeks the teams worked. They were meeting. And they were talking. But they couldn't move—paralyzed by having to work with strangers to make radical decisions and by the fear that steps in any direction would be wrong and they would fail.

Cross-functional work had to be learned as did a new way of thinking at Nissan. Japanese business principles and work habits were once the envy of the West and they are still closely regarded in Japan as the best way to get a job done. Very few, if any, outsiders have successfully walked into a large company in the country and gotten managers and executives to work in entirely new ways.

But Carlos Ghosn did.

A transformation began to take place after the first month among the Japanese middle managers who suddenly blossomed with hundreds of ideas, showing they in fact understood the challenge from the top ranks. Some even reveled in the opportunity to create and recommend ways the company could change. Says CFT pilot Shigeru Sakai: "We could not get started very quickly. Mr. Ghosn said, 'Just do it.' He asked everybody, 'What can you contribute to the company?'"

What can you contribute to the company? These were simple words from Ghosn, but words that had not been heard before in the middle management ranks of Nissan. Their job before was to react, not recommend. To work, not change. Upper-level management in conservative Japanese companies is not usually open to new ideas from the young and radical. So the concept that their recommendations were valid and respected was invigorating to managers once they understood there were no strings attached.

Solutions flowed, and when they were not aggressive enough, Ghosn pushed back from the top, making sure CFT leaders and pilots understood how far and deep he wanted them to look into the company for answers. Ghosn sent them back to planning sessions over and over again up until the very last minute of the third and final month, demanding more aggressive answers to Nissan's far-reaching problems. This push-review-push method started to take hold, and the middle lines of Nissan were speaking loud and clear as the three-month deadline steamrolled closer.

"Our initial anxiety was rather quickly relieved when it became obvious they had a lot to say," Klein says.

Concepts that many team members said openly at the start were not possible began to materialize—not just on paper, but in clear form in the minds of the executives and managers, who saw Nissan could in fact be turned around if aggressive, non-traditional action was taken. Costs could be cut. Ties could be broken.

"Three months was the longest time I could imagine," Ghosn says about the time granted CFTs. "Multitask work is simply a question of exercise. If you work on trying to act quickly, you'll be good at it. When you know that time is important, you learn to work faster. Of course, you should never adapt by skipping a process; you just learn to work faster."

Says Ghosn:

- If you work at trying to act quickly you become good at it.
- Never skip portions of the process when given a tight deadline; learn to work faster.

"We struggled in the beginning," says Kiyoaki Sawada, the general and administrative cost CFT pilot. "The area our team had to cover—reducing general and administrative costs—was so gray and wide that getting organized was difficult."

Sawada said matters were complicated by the fact that many members of his team had vastly different backgrounds, both from a cultural and business perspective, making communication difficult. "I only knew two members of the team," he says. "First we had to learn about each other. It was very, very difficult. Then, we started brainstorming. We took ideas to the executive committee. Mr. Ghosn wasn't satisfied . . . he wanted more aggressive ideas."

The mixing of managers from different cultures and disciplines on the CFTs created difficulties at first for some team members not used to working across such lines, but Ghosn insists that barriers like geographic boundaries are typically given more attention than deserved by corporations. The CFTs inspired managers to explore and discuss Nissan like never before. They found freedom through the cross-fertilization and eye-opening impact that the CFTs offered, and brainstormed their way to Ghosn-pleasing recommendations using Post-it notes and notebooks to gather the new ideas.

The nine CFTs completed the task in three months after assessing more than 2,000 ideas, ultimately presenting Ghosn and Nissan's executive committee with objectives ranging from new model launch and development to fewer suppliers to the closing of long-time Japanese manufacturing plants. Ghosn was satisfied, as were many CFT pilots and team members, who say the experience was an awakening of sorts for them, comparing it to boot camp, where new relationships and trust in one another is formed in the heat of the battle.

"Looking back, it was such an interesting and challenging time, not only for the company, but also for me," Sawada says. "Mr. Ghosn knew this, of course. He told us that each CFT member could have the personal experience of a lifetime."

Ghosn says the personal-growth result is one of the key elements of CFTs and that by reviving the spirit of key managers and employees it becomes a far more effective means of creating change than the typical method: a heavy ax falling from executive offices amid a scattered, isolated, and nonsupportive workforce.

Final recommendations from the nine CFTs were presented to Ghosn, Hanawa, and other members of the executive committee, creating a stir and debate over how far and how fast Nissan should move with its revival effort. Some argued that the company was frail and had already lost so much ground at home—a quarter century of market share decline in Japan— that breaking up the company's deeply woven keiretsu and closing manufacturing plants at the same time would be a final blow, causing domestic death by alienating last allies.

Ghosn, who had the final say, took all the CFT recommendations into consideration, knowing his actions would rock the foundation of Japan Inc. whether or not some controversial ones were left out of the company's revival plan. He considered the facts. He listened to reasons why some reform efforts should be delayed. Then he made a decision, creating one of the most aggressive and comprehensive restructuring efforts ever attempted by a manufacturing company the size of Nissan.

"It was a tough call," Ghosn says, "but I decided to go for it completely . . . the maximum level."

And the Nissan Revival Plan was born.

Ghosn was named Man of the Year by *Automobile Magazine* in January 2002 for turning Nissan around from near-bankruptcy to record profits. The award was presented in Detroit in conjunction with the annual North American Auto Show. Presenting the award is *Automobile Magazine* editor-in-chief Jean Jennings and Nissan's Debra Sanchez Fair.

Carlos Ghosn believes simple and clear are the cornerstones of good communication.

Nissan executives and senior managers say Ghosn is a keen listener who values input from all levels of the company. He arrived at Nissan with no preconceived notions about the company or Japan and listened to what others said before creating his action plan.

Ghosn earned the nickname "seven-eleven" in Japan for the long hours he worked during the formation of Nissan's revival plan. But away from the office, he concentrates on his children, often refusing to even read emails at home on weekends.

Norio Matsumura   Jed Connelly   Jim Morton

Shiro Nakamura · Tom Semple · Emil Hassan

Patrick Pelata

The 2003 350Z represents the birth of a totally new car that blends Nissan's sports car with cutting-edge technologies and a fresh design. The new Z has a base price of $26,269.

The 240Z debuted in the United States in 1970 and quickly became the fastest selling sports car in the world. The long-nosed rocket car became a symbol by which Nissan was known.

The Xterra was designed at Nissan Design America in San Diego and launched in 1999. The compact sport utility vehicle quickly became a Gen-X status symbol.

(*above*) The Altima was named 2002 North American Car of the Year and signaled Nissan's turnaround during its revival effort.

(*below*) The G35 sparked Infiniti sales and received rave reviews.

Ghosn and Mississippi governor, Ronnie Musgrove, found common ground when Nissan was looking for a site to build its new U.S. manufacturing plant. Canton, Mississippi, was chosen. Nissan's new full-size truck is one of several products to be built at the plant, opening summer 2003.

Nissan's Jed Connelly announced pricing on the 2003 350Z at the 2002 auto show in Detroit. The 350Z is priced similarly to the original 240Z that was first sold in the United States in 1970 when adjusted for inflation.

CHAPTER FIVE

Total Transparency Yields Trust

When Ghosn announced the much-anticipated Nissan Revival Plan (NRP) to the world in October 1999 he delivered a blow to postwar business Japan never seen before. This time, it was more than costs Carlos Ghosn was killing. The NRP, designed to immediately save millions and establish long-term growth opportunities to quickly return Nissan to respectability and profitability, cut deeply into Japanese cultural business tradition.

The aggressive plan was greeted by disbelief by many as longtime plant managers faced the realization that their jobs, along with thousands of workers under them, would be terminated—unheard of in Japan, the place where a job is supposed to be yours for life.

"[The Japanese] didn't like to make personnel changes," a longtime Nissan employee says. "If we needed to make cuts . . .

or a person wasn't doing a good job . . . it didn't matter. They hoped the problem would fix itself."

Even stock analysts who follow Nissan were shocked by the aggressive NRP and did little to buoy the stock, which fell more than 20 percent on the day of and the day after the announcement was made in Japan on the eve of the annual Tokyo Motor Show. Ghosn did not unveil the NRP amid one of the auto industry's biggest spectacles by accident. He knew the announcement would be heavily discussed and analyzed and felt the high-profile motor show would be the best moment to place all his cards on the table at the most public, visible time and place.

Ghosn had spent his three months on the job before the announcement fighting to keep bits of Nissan's plan-in-progress from reaching the media. He threatened all managers with their jobs if leaks continued to occur. In the final days, when Ghosn was making the hard decisions of exactly how far and deep to take the NRP, he talked with only a select few inside the company.

"I let everybody know that I would consider any leaks an act of sabotage against Nissan," Ghosn says. "It was important that pieces of information not get out so I could have an opportunity to fully explain details of the plan and why these changes were necessary."

The plan was so closely held that employees did not learn of its contents until the very moment Ghosn unveiled it publicly. Ghosn said during his speech that employees inside the company were learning about the NRP at the same time it was being announced publicly. He said members of the executive committee, absent from the public announcement, were explaining details of the plan internally while he met with members of the media.

- May 28, alliance transaction closed
- June 25, Nissan elects new Board of Directors
- June 25, Board appoints CEO, COO
- July 1, new executive management team officially starts work
- July 5, nine cross-functional teams formed
- October 18, NRP announced

Nothing to Hide

The silent period for Nissan ended when the NRP announcement began, ushering in a strategy that would be one of the most significant used by Ghosn in his effort to turn around Nissan: total transparency.

Ghosn believes corporations gain trust when motives and circumstances are clear rather than hidden. The temptation to avoid the truth in public is strong, especially when times get tough. That's why Ghosn and others talked so frankly about Nissan and its problems in the beginning, pinpointing problems in sometimes painful detail for all to see. Bluntly speaking the truth, no matter how harsh it sounds, became Ghosn's and Nissan's standard drill after the alliance. They figured if long-standing Japanese business traditions were to be broken, it was best others see exactly why such moves were being taken. Profit is the motive and no apologies are needed if management stands before consumers, employees, and shareholders in a crystal clear manner.

"Transparency is one of the most important issues facing business in the twenty-first century," he says. "We want to be completely transparent in everything we do at Nissan so there are no questions."

Taking Action

Transparency began in earnest when Ghosn made his now industry-famous NRP speech. One moment he was head of a struggling giant that had kept everyone, even most insiders, at a distance. A moment later, just in the time it took him to reach the podium and begin speaking, he broke down walls built over more than six decades, leaving public trust and integrity earned through honesty as Nissan's only shields.

"The key facts and figures about Nissan point to a reality: Nissan is in bad shape," Ghosn said at the beginning of the speech.

He had goose bumps when he walked to the podium in the packed ballroom to unveil the NRP, fully aware of the anticipation and implications that lay ahead. Speculation had been that a heavy ax would fall at Nissan soon after Renault announced that Ghosn would take over. Still, many were not prepared for the breadth of the NRP, which did far more than cut costs. Ghosn spoke for almost an hour, explaining NRP objectives with full reasoning.

The crowd was silent when he finished, but erupted in loud applause moments later. The news filtered quickly throughout the rest of Japan and other parts of the world, sending a message that Nissan would no longer be the same. The Nissan Revival Plan would start in fiscal year 2000 (beginning April 1, 2000) and last for three years—reducing debt, decreasing costs, and creating long-term growth opportunities.

NRP HIGHLIGHTS INCLUDED:

- Reduce operating costs by 1 trillion yen.
- Cut number of parts and materials suppliers in half.
- Reduce net debt from 1.4 trillion yen to less than 700 billion yen by FY 2002 (a reduction of $6 billion after the capital injection by Renault).
- Create new product investment and rollout, including launching of twenty-two new models by 2002.
- Reduce global head count by 21,000.
- Reduce number of vehicle assembly plants in Japan from seven to four.
- Reduce number of manufacturing platforms in Japan from twenty-four to fifteen.

"The combination of growth and cost reduction will allow Nissan to achieve a consolidated operating profit of 4.5 percent or more of sales by FY 2002," Ghosn said, a dramatic statement considering Nissan had lost money in seven of the past eight years and was used to negligible operating margins. There was also this fact to consider: cost reductions would not come without removing a significant chunk of Nissan's Japanese manufacturing operations.

Ghosn aimed to achieve the 1 trillion yen cost reduction in three major areas: global purchasing (breaking up keiretsu and asking for concessions from all suppliers); manufacturing; and general administrative costs. Three assembly plants in Japan were to be closed by March 2001, including Murayama (near Tokyo); Shatai Kyoto; and Aichi Kikai Minato. In addition, two power train operations, Kurihama Plant and Kyushu Engine Shop, were to be closed by March 2002. Worldwide jobs to be eliminated: 21,000, including more than 16,000 in Japan. The company with too many people building too few cars at too many plants in its home country was getting lean, doing the unwanted but logical.

For perspective, on the day the NRP was announced, Nissan's annual production of 1.28 million vehicles represented 53 percent of manufacturing capacity utilization, low by standards in any manufacturing industry. The goal of the NRP was to reduce capacity by 30 percent, raising the utilization rate to 82 percent by FY 2002. Auto plants, like hotels and restaurants, can't make profits operating at 50 percent capacity. Nissan had the ability in 1999 to manufacture up to 2.4 million vehicles, but only 1.3 million a year, or slightly less, were rolling off Japanese assembly lines and into the hands of consumers.

But no matter the logic of the NRP, some critics attacked Ghosn as the ruthless foreigner rattling a country already strained economically and emotionally. Some grumblings came in the media; others came from within, as a few managers resisted the changes and the headaches they knew would come with it. And some politicians, a year away from a general election in Japan, also made some noise as Nissan's massive job cuts added to the country's record unemployment.

Ghosn was undeterred, sticking to the mantra "We have no choice." He explained the need for Nissan's total reform to government leaders, industry insiders, and media types who would listen. He admitted the plant closures were painful but said the only way Nissan would ever regain productivity and profitability was through drastic measures within Japan. The decisions were tough, but Nissan had slipped away year after year by failing to address the problems it faced. Ghosn wasn't going to waste time placating others by tiered-in measures. He wanted it all done at once, proving to all that the company could be a vibrant corporate entity again.

Goodbye Keiretsu

Reducing purchasing costs by 20 percent was a major component of the NRP structure and arguably the most complex because of the ties that existed between Nissan and many suppliers. Reducing expenses may be the oldest management tactic in the book when profits dwindle and times get tough;

but the act was not as simple as it may sound for Nissan due to long-standing relationships.

Cutting costs and reducing capacity? Read Management 101 or quickly review any downsizing effort at a large Western company. Breaking up a Japanese keiretsu? Call Carlos Ghosn, who openly and aggressively tackled the integrated and tightly woven Japanese tradition when announcing the NRP.

The plan called for Nissan's purchasing to become centralized, following a scheme labeled "3-3-3" that would force Nissan's once-segregated purchasing and engineering divisions to work more closely with each other and with suppliers ("3-3-3" program means: 3 partners (suppliers, purchasing, and engineering), over 3 years, working in 3 regions (Asia, the Americas, and Europe/Middle East/Africa).

Ghosn said Nissan would reduce purchasing costs, representing 60 percent of the company's total operational costs, by 20 percent over the revival plan's three-year life, and the number of parts and materials suppliers would be cut almost in half, from more than 1,100 in 1999 to 600 or fewer by the end of 2002.

"This is a crucial objective, because purchasing represents 60 percent of our total costs, or a minimum of 58 percent of our net sales," Ghosn said. "Today, Nissan buys parts and materials on a regional basis, or even in certain areas on a country basis. This will stop immediately. Purchasing will be centralized and globalized."

Suppliers openly cringed at the thought of having to reduce costs by 20 percent in such a short period of time, but Ghosn promised that Nissan would help its partners meet the new objectives and also that suppliers making concerted efforts to lower costs would be rewarded with more business. It was a "you give some, we give some; you give more, you get more" approach to purchasing.

"We have too many suppliers," he said. "Overall, we will divide by two the number of suppliers to the Nissan group, which automatically means that our chosen suppliers, existing or new ones, will significantly increase their business with us."

"Speed is of the essence to us," Ghosn said. "That's why the first suppliers to clearly and credibly commit to the Nissan Revival Plan will be the first ones we will sign contracts with. This effort starts now, we will not wait."

Nissan would further reduce costs by centralizing global financial operations, reducing bureaucracy, and selling off non-core assets, such as land, securities—Nissan had shareholdings in almost 1,400 companies—and excess inventory. One example: in 1999 Nissan had $216 million invested in Fuji Heavy Industries, the maker of Subaru cars and trucks. Nissan was heavily invested in its own competitor yet its stake was not large enough to wield any leverage, making it a useless investment. Nissan could have used the money to develop new models that were badly needed. Instead, it was holding stock in a company that had nothing to offer.

"Our objective is to free resources from nonstrategic, non-core assets and invest more in our core business—cars—while at the same time significantly reducing our debt," Ghosn says. "Nissan had so much debt that it became almost impossible to invest in our future. Product development suffered."

Ghosn intended to reduce sales and general and adminis-trative costs 20 percent by cutting incentives, rationalizing worldwide advertising, and reducing bureaucracy, transforming Nissan from a multiregional organization into a truly global company.

Manufacturing Made Easy

Simplifying Nissan's complex manufacturing structure in Japan was a necessity and a major component of the NRP. The company was using twenty-four platforms, the backbone of a vehicle, at seven assembly plants in Japan when the plan was announced. Reducing the platforms to just fifteen at four plants by 2002 would help lower costs and speed production of new vehicles using the same platforms.

Nissan would also capitalize on its initial synergies developed through the cross-company teams with Renault where the companies determined it would be feasible and advisable to produce models in some markets on the same platforms. The challenge would be that both companies maintain separate identities, particularly in areas like design that make one automaker different from another.

The cost-saving benefits made simplified and shared manufacturing schemes seem like a natural move for both companies to benefit globally from the alliance. The objective was not to merge Renault with Nissan, but to find common ground when and where it makes sense while avoiding duplication. It was the first substantial public notice of how Renault and Nissan would begin to find global strength through the alliance. Designers from both companies could talk and share ideas, but they would not mingle vehicle-distinctive elements. Engineers, on the other hand, would work together to find ways to use the same platforms.

Building a Future

The NRP didn't stop at operational cost cutting and simplification measures. Significant new product rollout, brand development, and capital investment abroad were parts of the plan aimed at giving Nissan lasting profitable growth in the future, making the NRP more than a typical cost-savings plan.

"While cost cutting will be the most dramatic and visible part of the plan, we cannot save our way to success," Ghosn said.

Growth takes time to build, while cost reduction can be implemented immediately. Therefore, Nissan focused from the start of the NRP on rebuilding its brand, boosting research and development investment 25 percent while undergoing financial reform. Ghosn said Nissan needed to develop products that speak for themselves, building its brand through profits resulting from long-term consumer value and loyalty.

"I've heard a lot of speeches from car manufacturers about brand in the past and nothing's happened," Ghosn says. "We're going to do things differently; we're going to speak and show, and let the customer touch and feel as we're explaining what it is. At the end of the process they will not only understand the brand, but they can witness it in our products and our services."

Ghosn said Nissan would reduce its marketing costs by

"fighting against easy incentives" and "tackling issues that are usually difficult for a manufacturer, such as complexity and the reduction of everything that is not value added for the customer."

New Models

The new product-development segment of the NRP was crucial to Nissan's future, because, as Ghosn says, there's no problem in a car company that good products can't solve. And good products were lacking at Nissan when Renault took its stake in the company.

In all, Ghosn said Nissan would roll out twenty-two new models globally during its three-year NRP, including a number of new products in Japan. Reinventing current lines, as well as introducing new lines, such as the return of the once-popular Z car and the full-size pickup truck, debuting in 2003, allows Nissan products to sell at a premium, while potentially finding thousands of new customers along the way, particularly in the United States.

That's why the company's new plant in Canton, Mississippi—Nissan's billion-dollar gamble announced one year after the NRP—stands as an important piece of Nissan's future as Ghosn sees it. The new plant increases production in America soon after it was decreased in Japan. And workers in Mississippi will deliver Nissan's first-ever full-size truck, a product seen as an integral but somewhat risky, piece of the company's future. The Canton plant will also manufacture SUVs and minivans, all essentially new products for Nissan. (Until 2002, Nissan's U.S. minivan, Quest, was assembled by Ford Motor Company. The company also announced in 2002 that the Altima sedan will be built in Canton.)

"Today we do not participate in this very important segment—we're talking about more than two million units [sold per year] in the U.S. market," Ghosn said of full-size trucks. "And highly profitable. This will be the first time we will build our own minivan in the U.S. market. And we believe the market will support a full-size pickup. It's a major investment and the stakes are high . . . but we are focused."

Products Ghosn said Nissan would launch in North America under the NRP included:

- a new Q45 with a 4.5L V-8 engine sporting 340 horsepower
- the all-new Altima 2002 model with a V-6 engine option
- Sentra SE-R Spec V "pocket rocket"
- the Infiniti G35 sedan
- the reborn Z car (2003 model), a sorely needed image and traffic builder
- a new mid-size luxury performance Infiniti sedan called the M45
- the Infinity G35 Sport Coupe
- the new Nissan Murano, a unique crossover vehicle
- the FX45—Infiniti's version of a crossover SUV
- a redesigned all-new Maxima (2004 model)
- a redesigned all-new Quest (2004 model)

Ghosn said Nissan would survive short-term through the NRP's drastic cost-cutting, steps he knows many in Japan did not like but had no choice but to accept. He knew, though, that Nissan's long-term growth—its true revival—was dependent on the company's ability to generate customer excitement and loyalty like never before. "Product development will be at the heart of Nissan's revival," he said. "No doubt about it."

Other components of the NRP included:

- renewed emphasis on improved model design (Shiro Nakamura was introduced as Nissan's head of design) and reduced lead time getting a car to market
- simplified management structure
- performance-based compensation and advancement programs for management
- employee bonuses linked to global results

Ghosn was aware that the dramatic NRP would alienate many longtime Nissan allies, particularly those in Japan, but he said reforms were paramount to the company having any future at all, much less a bright one. It would be easier to do like so many other companies and tier in change, focusing on the reduction of labor costs one year; the reduction of purchasing costs the next; and the centralization of the treasury and management operations the next. But Ghosn wanted it all at once, telling others that short-term suffering would yield long-term reward.

"I know and I measure how much effort, how much sacrifice, and how much pain we will have to endure for the success of the Nissan Revival Plan," he said at the end of his NRP announcement. "But believe me, we don't have a choice, and it will be worth it."

A Promise to Deliver

Ghosn knew that simply making public plans for Nissan's revival would not be enough to convince media, shareholders, and the car-buying public that true change was on the way, due to the company's troubled past. The company famous for planning was announcing another plan. Been there and heard that. Tell me something new. A plan, even one drawn up with help from company employees, is no guarantee that a company will turn around. Doubters surfaced as soon as Ghosn began speaking, simply because history did not show it could be done fast, if at all.

George Wehrfritz wrote in *Newsweek International* shortly after the alliance (November 1, 1999) that turning money-losing Nissan into a profitable winner could take a couple of years at best: "Delays in unwinding Nissan's noncore assets, including land and shares in hundreds of Japanese companies, could put off profitability for two years or more. There's also doubt that Nissan's stale fleet of automobiles, many designed in the 1980s, can carry the company until new models are designed, produced and sent to showrooms, a two- to three-year pipeline. Add to this list worries about the strong yen and a possible downturn in the critical American export market and Ghosn's chances look only fair."

Ghosn knew this would be the case, inside the company and out. Announcing a plan was not enough. Management needed to commit, to make a promise that it would be different this time. And that's exactly what Ghosn did, making three commitments—promises—before everyone present for the NRP unveiling.

- a return to profitability for FY 2000, the NRP's first year
- a 50 percent decrease from the current net debt level by FY 2002
- an operating profit superior to 4.5 percent of sales by FY 2002

And he went farther, personally sticking himself and other members of Nissan's executive committee on the line. During a question-and-answer period following the NRP speech in which Ghosn made public management's three commitments, he was asked about making such a bold statement, promising profitability in 2000 when Nissan had lost money seven out of eight years. Was he prepared to accept responsibility for a company with such a poor track record?

Ghosn's response: If Nissan is not profitable in 2000, he and the rest of the executive committee will quit work and go fishing.

It was not a joke.

Nor was it a slip of the tongue.

Ghosn had not told fellow executive committee members he would make the public promise—that they would all quit if the company was not profitable in 2000—but the move was an effort to put management on the line at the same time that others were being asked to sacrifice for Nissan. The capacity crowd mumbled and stirred in their seats, soaking in the surprising words they had heard.

"Publicly I made three commitments," Ghosn says. "But to say Nissan will be profitable or I'll quit . . . this struck a chord. [Fellow] executive committee members were obviously surprised when they heard of my remark."

It was a deeply calculated risk Ghosn considered worth taking because he believed analysts and members of the media in attendance needed to see something different in Nissan and its leaders.

No more vague remarks.

No more empty promises.

We will do as we say or else we will personally pay the price along with the company and its shareholders. Transparent, bold talk rarely heard in Japan Inc., where even the obvious is discussed in a sideline manner. The remark made headlines all over the world and has been mentioned in almost every feature article written about Ghosn and Nissan since. More important, it was a major turning point inside the company.

"I knew exactly what I was doing and what kind of risk I was taking," Ghosn says. "They were saying, 'He's been on the job here just three months and he's making that kind of commitment, we can do the same.' It was the best way I knew how to say clearly: We are going to do this and get results."

We will do this or we will quit.

Bam.

The Nissan Revival Plan launched like a rocket.

CHAPTER SIX

The Art of Implementation

Ghosn did not have to quit his job. Neither did fellow members of the executive committee. Nissan was not only profitable in fiscal year 2000; the company posted its highest profits in corporate history.

What a difference a year makes.

Doubters would fade away if Nissan proved them wrong by posting dramatic results during the first year of its revival plan, Ghosn said. They might not like how it was done or why it was done, but the quickest way to silence critics and make believers out of consumers and shareholders was with quick, striking results nobody could argue with.

That's why Ghosn could barely contain his enthusiasm when he went to the podium in May 2001 to announce that Nissan had produced its best financial performance in the company's history for fiscal year 2000 (ending March 31, 2001), the first year of the NRP. He had goose bumps when he announced the NRP. This time, he had a handful of figures that showed Nissan was in fact headed in a new direction.

The company earned 290 billion yen in net income just one year after its worst year ever. The revival effort got an early start due to the cross-company work occurring beforehand, but there was still no mistaking the difference in one year on the corporate calendar. "I begged our employees for their full support and active involvement," he said. "This is their answer to you today."

Implementing the Plan

Establishing the plan and making public tough initiatives to reform Nissan made international headlines, but Ghosn and others inside the company knew that revival and renewed confidence depended totally on swift and effective implementation of the NRP.

Nissan's previous turnaround efforts in the 1990s failed because the plans were never followed company wide and often were changed shortly after announcement, when politics and tradition got in the way. Now, an outsider was attempting change and doing things that weren't exactly acceptable in the company's home country. The only solution was to earn quick credibility through head-turning results.

Ghosn was aware that skeptics doubted whether he and his team of Renault expats stood any chance at breaking up Nissan's keiretsu and winning over longtime employees who did not want change within the company's Japanese framework. There was also this factor: planning global change, at any company, is much easier than actually doing it. And, undoubtedly, an old, conservative automaker, built on totally separate foundations on different continents, would be harder than others to transform.

The Japanese had built a cocoon around Nissan's Tokyo operational center, making it difficult for new ideas to flow in and out, and the NRP was all about one great, big idea: returning Nissan to short-term and long-term profitability. Momentum had already shifted toward change in many corners of Nissan in the months just before the NRP was announced due to energy created by the cross-company and cross-functional teams. But once the plan was revealed company wide, Ghosn made it clear where daily job emphasis should lie: implementation of the Nissan Revival Plan.

Pushing for the plan to be put into action became his biggest daily focus after the NRP announcement was made. Some call implementation his obsession; others say it is more a matter of fact in that he knows that change cannot occur without precise implementation of the plan.

It was easier said than done in Japan, where new business practices are not easily accepted. Japanese businessmen typically like change to occur slowly over long periods of time. Ghosn was asking them to bring down great walls built over decades practically overnight.

"[Ghosn] is a very operational type of leader," says Philippe Klein, a Nissan vice president and former Renault executive who played a key role in the revival effort as Ghosn's "operations" right hand. "If we are not *doing* the plan, it means nothing to him. A lot of CEOs have visions, but he has an ability to look at single-action plans . . . he puts all of his emphasis on implementation."

He got Japanese managers and executives to do it by insisting they change the way they worked, spending more time on getting the job done than talking about the job to be done. There was no time to hash and rehash consequences and potential results, allowing change to occur over a much slower and more palatable period suitable for the Japanese.

The people had been empowered to *create* the plan; now they had to *do* the plan.

Akira Sato, the finance vice president who has worked for Nissan for more than twenty years, is one of many who say Ghosn and the urgent demands of revival made them reprioritize and learn new daily work habits. Sato was a CFT pilot, directing the finance cost team, and was responsible for implementing the NRP in his role in the company's treasury department. He was pushed to plan in a shorter time period than he was used to; then told to do nothing but implement until told otherwise. It was a new but effective way of working that got Nissan moving.

"Before [Ghosn] arrived, we spent probably 60 percent of our time planning," Sato says. "But Mr. Ghosn told me, 'Use five percent of your time planning and ninety-five percent on implementation.' It is a Japanese people's behavior, to want to plan all the time. But this time we focused on one objective. In my case, it was to reduce assets . . . but everybody within the company began to focus on implementation of the plan."

Ghosn does not see daily harping on implementation as either an obsession or as a part of his job, but as necessity, the fundamental difference between revival and failure.

"First, you have to give employees the opportunity to create change by discussing and listening at all levels of the company," he says. "Then you have to decide and implement. It can be easy and useless to spend too much time listening and planning without effective implementation."

He understands that the notion that a company and individuals within it should focus "ninety-five percent on execution and delivery" and "five percent on planning" sounds ridiculous, because it is so logical. Yet, he says, planning is often where more time is spent within a company if top management is not clear in its directives and if it does not insist that the job get done, now. Employees will talk and plan and talk and plan until the company is so far behind in reaching its objectives that new plans are needed.

"We're a business," Ghosn says. "What people see is what we execute. Part of my Latin surroundings is an ability to talk too much and not implement. I've seen it in many places, actually—Brazil, France, and Italy—where people tend to think about a problem and talk about it . . . without doing anything about it. The temptation to talk is so big. I consider it pleasant on a personal level; extremely unpleasant in business."

Nissan's focus on implementation paid off. Just nineteen months after Ghosn announced the NRP and said Nissan was in bad shape he was standing before many of the same media members to announce that the company was not ready to cast off its underdog role, but had moved decisively from "the emergency room to the recovery room," posting its best financial results in the history of the company.

Nissan was on the move, reviving faster than anyone other than even the most optimistic could have imagined. Sales increased in fiscal year 2000 by 4 percent (though short-term growth wasn't an NRP objective); the first handful of twenty-two new products was launched; management was streamlined; purchasing costs were reduced by 11 percent (more than half of the total NRP goal was achieved in one year); manufacturing utilization rates in Japan increased from 51 percent to 74 percent; and the company earned 5.4 percent operating income on sales, by far the best margin in its history.

The turnaround from one year to the next was dramatic and proof that Nissan employees implemented at a furious pace, eliminating noncore assets, centralizing global financial operations, breaking up the keiretsu, benchmarking, building brand identity, focusing on profitable business, developing exciting new products, and changing the way employees were managed and compensated.

No Ghosts

Nissan had a lot of problems before the alliance, but none got public attention like its mountain of debt, making the elimination of noncore assets a vital NRP component. The company could not be profitable while serving billions of dollars in debt. The answer was the reduction of hundreds of nonessential holdings accumulated through the years, such as the $216 million investment in the maker of Subaru cars and trucks.

In all, Nissan had shares in 1,394 companies before the NRP, including a stake of 20 percent or more in half of those. Nissan would continue holding shares in only four of those companies, Ghosn said.

Sales of land and securities began immediately, but only at fair prices; not at fire-sale levels. Since Nissan was the beneficiary of the $5.4 billion cash infusion it was not desperate to sell anything for less than a fair price. Management made it clear they were in a selling mode but that nothing would be dispensed of in a knee-jerk way. But with only a small handful of exceptions, all of Nissan's holdings were marked dispensable. The sales process began almost immediately after the NRP was announced.

Akira Sato helped create Nissan's revival plan as a CFT pilot, making recommendations to the executive committee that holdings be massively reduced. Then he was asked to put the plan into action—an unenviable job for a man who had worked at Nissan and lived in Japan most of his life. He laughs at the thought today; at the realization that he played a major role in churning and changing the business landscape in his country in such a dramatic way. But the laugh is a nervous one, a sign that the soft-spoken man of finance has not forgotten the pains that came with implementation.

Nissan had longtime, interwoven relationships with several hundred of the companies in which large stakes were held. Some of the relationships dated back fifty years or more and were bound by the ties of Japan Inc., making personal visits necessary to explain why Nissan was divesting share ownership.

Sato visited with many of the more than 300 companies Nissan had close relationships with, delivering the news that change was imminent and holdings would be sold. It was not easy, even though the action was necessary.

Nissan was paralyzed by too many investments that did not generate cash flow, hindering research and development in key emerging markets like China. It didn't matter when Japan's economy steamrolled along in the 1970s and 1980s and practically all credible manufacturing companies experienced dramatic growth. But when Japan's economic bubble burst in the 1990s, holding shares in nonperforming companies made less sense and Nissan paid the price, borrowing money while clinging to old, nonessential business relationships.

Sato knew this—he recommended it as a CFT pilot—but actually doing it, breaking up links that had existed for dozens of years by looking longtime associates in the eyes, took some courage.

Financial reform is one thing.

Breaking up a traditional web of Japanese business is another.

Sato says presidents of almost every company he visited complained about Nissan's move to sell off holdings in non-essential companies and resorted to political persuasion in efforts to stop or slow down the plan. Nissan was told it would further damage the sick Japanese economy, pushing share prices down further with large block sales. Some threatened that Nissan would be damaged the same way in return. What is good for one is good for another, and these companies promised to sell Nissan shares in return, creating less market value for all. But Nissan was selling noncore assets for long-term stability. Management stuck to the plan despite the protests and never wavered in its commitment to get rid of shareholdings that made no sense for the automaker to own.

"It was very difficult because they very strongly rejected our plan," Sato says. "[Nissan's] old management would have told me to wait and postpone action because they were focused on the [Japanese] relationship. But I did not have to pay attention to complaints because new management was focused. So I visited companies and tried to convince them this action would help revive Nissan. We went forward."

Sato, who says he knew at the time he was making Japanese business history by breaking up a Japanese keiretsu, gained confidence with each passing day of the process, realizing that Nissan, and more specifically, Japan Inc., would not only survive the change; it would be far better off in the end, able to stand stronger on the global front on its own merit. Domestically there would be short-term pains; long-term there would be international gains.

"In the past," he says, "people would say that if we cross this line, a ghost will come out. But we did cross it and . . . no ghosts."

Centralizing the Treasury

Nissan's internal financial reform tasks were met with similar displeasure because global centralization of the company's money meant less regional management clout. Before the NRP, Nissan was structured globally as separate regional entities. Each division president in each country managed bank accounts and financial data.

The result: Nissan dealt with 200 banks worldwide.

The company was able to reduce that number to just fifteen through the NRP, but not without long discussion and a strong arm. Going to the division leaders and telling them financial controls were being taken away wasn't much easier than going to outside companies to break the news that relationships were ending. "Each president had his own castle," Sato says. "They wanted to manage it by themselves."

The reason, for argument's sake, was that by holding accounts according to world regions, long-term relationships could be developed that were beneficial to Nissan. This was no doubt true to an extent. But the CFT financial and cost findings were clear: Nissan was paying too much to manage its own money and the advantages of centralization outweighed those being gained from local and regional leverage.

Nissan's Tokyo headquarters was designated the company's global treasury and dozens of accounts throughout the world were closed and consolidated, a first step in the globalization of the company. The result was less punch locally; more power globally.

"We had a lot of meetings with [division presidents]," Sato says. "Some, obviously, did not like the idea at all. We had to tell them the expected effect—that we would experience significant cost reduction."

The global treasury consolidation reduced Nissan's financial operational costs from 90 billion yen in 1999 to just 24 billion yen quickly because less direct expense was needed in the way of manpower and fees. But although the global treasury operates out of Tokyo that doesn't mean Japanese banks always get the business. Nissan's quest to find partners that meet worldwide needs has caused grumblings that the company is eliminating some Japanese banks from participating with a large Japanese manufacturer by seeking financial partners that offer global solutions.

Sato keeps his eye on corporate goals, understanding that banks, like corporations, must take a global view in light of changing economic conditions in the country. "Money is money," he says. "So, centralized management makes sense for everybody. It just makes sense. It was an old idea, but we did not implement it before. Ghosn pushed us to implement. We had to challenge the staff, but we did it because Nissan was in the dark . . . I could feel the sense of urgency."

Suppliers Forced to Change

Parts suppliers have traditionally been "under the umbrella" of the Japanese automakers, so when Nissan announced it was reducing purchasing costs by 20 percent over three years; cutting the number of suppliers it used in half; and opening the door to new global contracts that met specifications, all time-honored rules of the supplier-manufacturer relationship, in Nissan's case, at least, were off the table.

Ghosn essentially put all of Nissan's 1,100-plus suppliers on notice when he declared in his NRP speech that the first ones with credible ideas for achieving the company's new objectives would be rewarded with contracts. The comments were a deliberate and calculated effort to make suppliers he anticipated would be slow to offer early, concrete solutions rush to seize the promise of new opportunity. He stressed that only suppliers working in the best interests of Nissan would be partners in the future but that the favor would be returned by more business and help in finding cost-cutting solutions.

The management team that came to Nissan from Renault did not have a lot of sympathy for Nissan suppliers because they felt that business relationships are not good if both parties do not mutually benefit. Nissan, in this case, was hurting since it was determined during the CFT study phase that the company was paying for many parts at premiums much greater than competitors were paying for the same parts. Nissan was certainly due its share of the blame, having allowed prices to rise through the years without challenge. That is why the company promised to help, telling suppliers they would not be isolated in their efforts to find savings.

"In 1999 we were told that by cutting twenty percent we would kill the supply base," Klein says. "We told them it would not be easy, but we would work with them."

Some suppliers quickly jumped on Ghosn's offer, lowering prices and working with Nissan engineers to find less expensive ways to do business. Company specifications were changed in some cases and prices were simply lowered in others as suppliers worked to forge relationships with Nissan's new management team and capture a share of the promise of more business in the future. Other suppliers talked about change but were slow to give concrete proposals and were among the ones eliminated from Nissan's overgrown base.

This, more than any other aspect of the revival plan, had the most to do with Nissan's quick turnaround in financial results, since purchasing gobbled up so much of the company's operating budget. It is also an area where Ghosn's previous experience made a direct impact on how it was done. At Michelin, he had worked for a supplier, learning the relationship from the other side for years. When he moved to Renault, his supplier-based knowledge was a factor in the company's restructuring effort, which reduced purchasing costs.

His secret is that he relies heavily on benchmarking, comparing costs against other companies in the industry. Companies around the world that are doing well are using benchmarking as a big competitive advantage. Ghosn says full-scale, up-to-date benchmarks are the only way a company can know if good buys are being made. In Nissan's case, the purchasing CFT and its subteams—consisting of executives and managers from purchasing, engineering, manufacturing, and finance—had a distinct advantage during NRP deliberations: complete access to Renault purchasing information.

Nissan got many things from Renault when the alliance was signed, like Ghosn and a check for $5.4 billion. But the effective use of comparative purchasing information was a strategic advantage. Seeing is believing, and many suppliers and Nissan managers and executives needed black-and-white proof that they were paying way too much. Ghosn knew Nissan was paying suppliers too much. But he also knew it was not as simple as him saying, stop. Managers and executives charged with making purchasing decisions need fact-based information for persuasion.

Benchmarking had worked for Ghosn at Michelin North America when the company experienced turbulent times shortly after its acquisition of Uniroyal-Goodrich. Michelin managers took advantage of records from the newly acquired company and the factual, comparative base of information eliminated many potential purchasing turf battles.

Ghosn directed a similar but more comprehensive effort at Nissan. Members of the purchasing CFT looked directly at Renault's records for comparative prices on literally hundreds of parts and supplies, as the French company held nothing back from its new Japanese ally. "Our one big advantage," he says.

Renault purchasing documents revealed that Nissan was getting robbed, paying premiums ranging from 25 to 40 percent on practically every part it purchased. Immediately there were cries within Nissan that comparing parts costs in Europe to those in Japan wasn't fair, due to value-added advantages from trading in-country. But engineers who had operated with autonomy at Nissan before the NRP, making their own determinations of which parts and suppliers would be used, were now answering to purchasing and finance, working in cross-functional cohesion. The absence of departmental barriers removed by the cross-work of the CFTs made it difficult for one discipline to argue against any cost-cutting measures without providing fact-based backup information.

It's a management game Ghosn loves to play, creating intra-company transparency where only the facts survive. He loves it when data and analysis win and loses his patience when individuals persistently argue a point with nothing to back it up.

"A benefit of benchmarking is questioning your own performance based on facts," Ghosn says. "It's a very powerful tool, especially when dealing with engineering. If I benchmark, and do it properly, these are facts my engineers cannot ignore."

Simply asking within the company if it is "purchasing well" is not effective management. The answers are predictable.

"They say, 'I think so,'" Ghosn says. "Then, we take a look at maybe fifty items on one vehicle, and we determine others in our industry are paying discounts of twenty-five percent or more on parts all across the board . . . they can't tell me they are doing the best they can do. We had Renault to compare with in the beginning, but we will continue to look in other areas, at other companies."

Implementing the 20 percent cost reductions called for in the NRP was more political than painful to Nissan. The company was eliminating almost half of its current supplier base and demanding that those remaining help reduce purchasing costs companywide by *at least* 20 percent in three years or less. Ghosn made it clear this issue was nonnegotiable, that solutions had to be found, no matter what. He offered suppliers help in return, promising that Nissan engineers would work on teams with suppliers through the 3-3-3 initiative, searching for ways both companies could improve efficiency and profitability, regardless of the reductions.

Ghosn told Nissan engineers that one-third of the cost reductions could be achieved through changes to company engineering specifications that he believed were stricter than those of other automakers. Nissan wasn't about to compromise quality for consumers, but Ghosn pointed out that simplified specifications, in many instances, could deliver the same quality at lower costs. He gives an example of headlamps Nissan engineers were using prior to NRP. The headlamps, according to specifications, had parts standards higher than those of competitors, though the differences were so minuscule customers had no performance benefit from the enhancement. A couple of minor adjustments to components such as reflectors and panels within the headlamps decreased costs 2.5 percent. Suppliers on the part had not yet made any concessions but costs were already decreased. All that had to be done was to change the internal mindset—and specifications.

The findings are just one example of direct, internal cost-saving opportunities uncovered by the CFTs. How they were found—through cross-functional work—made implementing the changes easier for engineers and others who could not argue the work done by teams of colleagues. What seemed impossible before was now presented in undeniable fashion.

Purchasing costs were also reduced by the company's global strategy. Purchasing, just like the treasury, had been run on a regional basis before the NRP, resulting in little or no worldwide buying clout.

"Our headquarters function was rather weak," Sato says.

Itaru Koeda, Nissan's executive vice president in charge of purchasing (he also oversees European operations), has the task of working with major suppliers who are trying to meet Nissan's new requirements. He says Nissan packs more power by purchasing from headquarters in larger quantities from fewer suppliers. The downside, in Japan at least, is that many suppliers who wanted to maintain business with Nissan not only had to reduce costs, but provide solutions in all areas of the country, since partners with worldwide vision were wanted. The goal of the NRP is to revive Nissan, but also to create a more firm foundation for long-term success through the creation of a seamless, global company: one brand, one mission.

"We used to be a Japanese company with major operations in the United States and Europe," Koeda says. "Now, Nissan is a global company. Purchasing is a major part of this."

Complaints were many in the beginning of the NRP—particularly from Japanese companies with long-standing Nissan relationships—but the volume of complaints subsided substantially once suppliers understood the necessity to change and the results that were possible—on both sides.

"We try to make them understand by referring to our benchmarking," Koeda says. "There are not many disputes over benchmark results. We are willing to work with them, bringing together engineering, suppliers, and purchasing to find solutions. Many understand."

Some do not, no longer doing business with Nissan; one or two even went out of business. Those that have adapted, following Nissan in its centralization and globalization effort, are finding new markets, greater profits, and greater potential ahead as Nissan grows. "Some [suppliers] are struggling," Sato says. "Others can now see the blue sky and wider business opportunities outside of Japan. They are seeing beyond Nissan and trying to be more global."

The Alliance Finds Strength in Numbers

Nissan and Renault made it clear when the alliance was signed that global strength for both companies would come from binational, cross-company work benefiting both. The alliance was not a takeover where the buyer abuses the brand of the other to its own benefit; nor was it designed to be a dictatorship, with one calling the shots over the other. It was founded purely on the basis of synergy, the belief that two steps forward together is better than one using the other as merely a stepping-stone.

One way the companies benefit mutually is through a joint

purchasing company that was formed. The Renault Nissan Purchasing Organization is an oddity of sorts and representative of the alliance in general because of its unique nature. Why? The organization buys for two companies that operate separately and maintain ongoing purchasing reduction plans.

Renault, after all, had just completed its three-year cost-cutting plan that was initiated by Ghosn. Nissan was in the midst of its plan to reduce purchasing costs by at least 20 percent. Here came another purchasing entity charged with creating dual buying strength through shared parts and supplies. A main office was opened in Paris with satellite offices in Japan and Europe. The global purchasing organization helped Renault and Nissan save an additional 1 percent or more per year in purchasing costs.

For Nissan, this was above and beyond what the company was striving for through the NRP and proof that alliance synergy was not just talk. By moving toward shared platforms and similar manufacturing schemes the visionaries of the alliance were seeking to capitalize on strengths in numbers that benefit both Nissan and Renault.

Getting New Models to Market

Getting new products to market quicker than ever before was a critical element of the NRP because Nissan is an automaker and automakers talk about the exciting and saleable qualities of the vehicles they make.

A problem, though, was that Nissan had very little to talk about at the time of the alliance in terms of new and exciting products. The media just wanted to discuss Nissan's dismal financial situation and previous management problems, creating a communications challenge, since Ghosn did not want to continue harping on the company's past. Yes, he wanted to identify the problems and address them head-on, but he was anxious for something new to talk about—like a new Z car.

The communications strategy was to first talk about what would be done, then divert attention with quick, striking results. But Nissan's new management team knew those tactics would only last so long and that eventually the company had to be noticed for the exciting, new products it designed and built.

"We had to talk about what we were going to do," Klein says. "The strategy was to quickly restore credibility through profitability and with our product lineup."

Nissan was notoriously slow by industry standards in getting new models to market in the decade before the alliance. It took the company twelve to eighteen months in the 1990s to start the sales of a new car in a foreign market after it was launched first in Japan, causing Nissan to have to offer more incentives in the foreign markets while "waiting for an already known replacement." The company that was once a trendsetting leader in the industry was being zoomed by.

One way Nissan sped up model development was by reducing the number of platforms that were being used. The development of a new car from an existing platform takes 30 to 50 percent less time than developing a new car from an all-new platform, so this move was a natural for Nissan (in addition to other cost-saving benefits of reduced platforms).

Also, Shiro Nakamura was fully empowered as head of design, receiving in some cases unheard-of authority over engineers and freedom to move swiftly and freely in tackling the more than thirty new products under consideration, including entirely new products, new derivative products, and enhanced existing products. Ghosn hired Nakamura away from Isuzu in 1999 to become Nissan's chief designer because he knew that financial reform was only one of the keys to survival. Revival, and ultimately growth, depended upon new, exciting products as well.

Nakamura, an artist and musician who has worked in the United States and Europe, is a car enthusiast who dreamed as a young boy in Japan of creating vehicles that would be driven and admired all over the world. He has been in the business a long time, but he still displays a childlike enthusiasm when talking about cars, particularly the new models coming from Nissan. His passion and likeable flair have elevated him to minor celebrity status in Japan. The company has even used him in car ads in Japan, significant considering Nissan lets products speak for themselves, rarely using people in marketing campaigns.

"I had heard talk that Nissan was conservative and bureaucratic," Nakamura says. "There were some good designs in the studio, but for different reasons they were not coming to production."

One of the first changes at Nissan's technical center on the outskirts of Tokyo where Nakamura and his team of designers create were completely remodeled facilities, reflecting the ultrachic tastes of the new head designer. Nissan was strapped for cash and operating under an aggressive, cost-cutting revival plan yet Ghosn approved the renovation despite dated décor at the company's Tokyo headquarters facilities—a move in direct opposition to the way the company had been run before.

The reasoning was clear: Ghosn believed new, exciting products delivered in record time would save the company.

Nakamura, who keeps a hallway at the facility filled with the latest and innovative Japanese art he finds, says the renovation, coming in a difficult time, showed his team management was serious about styling, unleashing two-and-a-half years of creativity in volumes he had never seen before. Nakamura works closely with U.S. designers at Nissan Design America (NDA), based in San Diego, to meet the demands of Nissan's postalliance, frenetic production pace by creating market-specific cars in global fashion. The results: a new Z-car, the full-size truck, a new sports utility, the new Altima, a new minivan, the Murano cross-over vehicle—more than two dozen new or radically changed models emerging from dream to reality.

"Amazing," he says.

Nissan Design America is home to sixty of the fewer than 500 automotive designers in all of North America. The designers work closely with engineers at the Nissan Technical Center North America (NTCNA) located just outside of Detroit, and Nakamura in Tokyo, to find regional designs reflecting world vision and unified design reflecting the brand's "Nissan-ness."

The U.S. design center was started in 1979 as Nissan Design International by former chief designer Jerry Hirshberg, who created a secluded, hillside retreat that intentionally fostered unorganized and unorthodox ways of working. Designers at the U.S. design studio were so removed from normal work routines that lunchtime volleyball games and even a movie break or two during work hours helped spur creativity.

Semple is a former GM designer who joined Hirshberg at the design studio in 1980. He took over in 1999 when Hirshberg retired shortly after the alliance was formed and change occurred as fast as the NRP was developed. The name was changed to Nissan Design America and new approaches to work and design were introduced, reflective of the company's new global view and short production calendar. Some NDA designers keep their skills sharp working on nonautomotive products ranging from a 150-foot yacht to preschool furniture and golf clubs. Freedom still exists, as do on-site tennis and volleyball courts, but the frantic design pace and increased responsibility for designers has lessened exotic work time.

Because of the company cross-work instituted under Ghosn, designers are involved in models throughout the life of the car, since engineering changes and marketing demands directly affect design. Designers now talk daily with team members in Japan, Europe, and North America and frequently meet with teams from engineering and sales and marketing. The increased involvement means more work, but the changes are welcomed by most designers, who recognize the challenge given by Ghosn—a license to create all-new vehicles that reflect an emerging innovative brand—is a designer's. They know their work gives management something to talk about besides a troubled past.

Investing in a Future

The new pipeline of products means that Nissan needed more manufacturing capacity in the right places. The natural assumption would be that a company in a massive cost-restructuring would cut or delay long-term investments until better financial times.

Not postalliance Nissan.

The company's new billion-dollar plant in Mississippi was announced just one year after the NRP because Ghosn believed building the right products at the right time and place was critical to Nissan's future. The Canton plant allows Nissan to build more models in the United States, where profits and future demand are solid. It also creates more production balance between America and Japan, eliminating the cost of transporting exported units overseas.

Nissan made its selection of Mississippi for its new North American plant the same way it has done everything else after Ghosn arrived—fast. Sites were narrowed to four southeastern locations and Canton, Mississippi, was among them. Mississippi governor Ronnie Musgrove said the first meeting he ever held with Nissan involved Carlos Ghosn, something not usually done by top corporate executives. Most companies send other executives in first during site location, but Ghosn wanted to see and discuss firsthand.

"This was different than what a lot of company leaders do," Musgrove says.

Musgrove says Ghosn talked about business philosophies and his vision for Nissan more than he talked about specifics of Mississippi and its ability to build quality cars during the first meeting. "He talked about the last twenty-nine years of business at Nissan," he says. "He shared his vision for the company."

Musgrove, in return, shared his vision of Mississippi, about how it was often the last on lists ranking the fifty states. "There was no need to sugarcoat the truth," he says. "But I found striking parallels between his vision and mine. We had some common ground."

The catch was that Nissan, in its hyperspeed mode,

needed the state to have its incentives package, land availability, and workforce demographics put together in just a handful of months. The typical site selection process for a plant the size of the one Nissan was planning to build is twelve to eighteen months, but Ghosn said it had to be done in roughly six months to meet production demands.

Nissan had no time to waste. Musgrove obliged, saying Mississippi would get it done, "no ifs, ands, or buts."

The proposal was put together and hand-delivered to Ghosn at Nissan North America's headquarters in Los Angeles (he was on another trip and had stopped in Los Angeles before flying on to Tokyo). Musgrove gave him the proposal, along with a cell phone that had been preprogrammed to call from Tokyo directly to the governor's home in Mississippi if the state was selected for Nissan's new manufacturing plant.

The cell phone rang just a few weeks later.

"It was a watershed moment for Mississippi, no doubt about it," Musgrove says.

For Nissan, it was another major step forward in a fast race to implement plans that were long overdue.

Building Brand Identity

Once vehicles are designed and built, the price they command from consumers—the key to strong profits—is directly related to the strength of a company's brand.

Nissan's showroom power was clearly deficient before the alliance. Building brand identity isn't seen with the same importance by many large companies in Japan as it is in the United States and other Western countries. That's why Nissan had given little effort in the 1990s to establishing a global brand image, the promise a brand makes to a customer. Brand identity was created in the past as more of a by-product, not through a unified, corporate, global effort.

Nissan was considered innovative at one time when products like its old Z car created a promise of style and quality, particularly in the United States. It also sponsored sports teams in Japan and made isolated image-building efforts. But Nissan's brand image had suffered dreadfully beginning in the mid-1990s when outdated and limited product lineups failed to deliver innovation and the company wasn't putting forth cohesive messages worldwide.

The result was that Nissan products sold at lower prices compared to competitive cars in all major markets. The sales price deficiencies were estimated to be $1,000 in the United States; 700 euros in Europe; and a minimum of 40,000 yen per car sold in Japan. The wasted margins were the difference between red and black numbers on the corporate balance sheet, enough to make building a stronger global brand identity a top company goal.

"Many companies in Japan see no need to make an effort to give a particular message to the marketplace," says Norio Matsumura, Nissan's executive vice president of global sales and marketing.

Nissan was known as a technologically advanced automaker in Japan at one time, when it owned market share in Japan in the 1960s and early 1970s and when it brought its hot-selling sports cars to the United States. But Nissan, like most Japanese companies, used its products to speak to customers. When that no longer worked the brand suffered the consequences, since no unified corporate marketing messages were being distributed worldwide. The result was that buyers were paying an average of $1,000 more for Toyota products with similar specifications.

During the NRP's first year, a global brand identity strategy was planned and put into action, sending the same core messages about Nissan's new bold and innovative products and approach.

Matsumura is in charge of what is Nissan's first true global marketing function. One of the first challenges was to make sure employees understood the new brand image and why developing it is important to the company's success. The solution: more than 4,000 employees in Japan, Europe, and North America were put through training to help the company leverage efforts in building its brand.

"There were no clear lines between sales and marketing at Nissan in the past," says Shiro Tomii, Nissan's senior vice president of marketing in Japan. "Each department had direction, but they were separate, not working together. Under the NRP we make sure: one company, one message."

Focusing on Profits, Not Sales

Another way of ensuring profits on sales is by not following the lead set by American manufacturers of giving deep incentives too often.

Nissan operated under the mindset before the alliance that

putting vehicles on the roads at any cost was more important than selling them at profitable levels. This was part of the same notion that closing plants wasn't acceptable. Plants and people make cars; sales and marketing must find a way to dish them off, no matter the cost, so that plants do not have to be closed.

But the management view after the alliance was that healthy companies are highly profitable companies and healthy companies hire more people. If a company wants to create jobs in the long-term it must operate as profitably as possible in the short-term.

When Nissan was hurting it relied on incentives to motivate customers, selling its car below the premiums other manufacturers demanded. In the United States, leased vehicles were often given artificially high residual values, allowing customers to drive cars at lower monthly payments. This put more cars on the road but kept the company from making money or breaking even. Ghosn told Nissan's global sales and marketing executives shortly after arriving that Nissan should never strive for market share it "did not earn" and made it clear that products should be sold profitably or not sold at all.

They listened. During NRP implementation Nissan's market share climbed incrementally, while its profitability soared. Nissan fought the temptation to offer deep incentives for extended periods of time, as U.S. automakers have grown accustomed to doing, and watched profits on specific models go higher.

"Mr. Ghosn talks to us about market presence, not market share," says Jed Connelly, Nissan's senior vice president of sales and marketing. "It's easy to buy market share, but you have to earn a strong presence. We believe that once we reestablish

Nissan as a strong presence, market share will follow naturally. If we can't make money selling a product, we don't want to do it just to have vehicles on the road."

Steps were taken to restructure management in ways that ensured that each model Nissan produces is watched daily for ways to enhance profitability and solve problems that might lower profitability. "How many cars did we sell last month?" was never the first question out of Ghosn's mouth when talking to executives at Nissan North America during implementation of the NRP. He simply wanted to know if models were being sold profitably and if steps were being taken to follow other components of the plan.

Changing Within

Restructuring personnel and management schemes within the company might have been Nissan's biggest challenge, fundamentally, considering the cultural aspects of the change in Japan. Thousands of jobs were to be eliminated, plants closed, and compensation and management schemes restructured at the highest levels.

Every single move was in direct opposition to Japanese business traditions, causing headaches for the human resource department in Tokyo, which essentially managed only Japan before the NRP, since HR schemes at Nissan were distinct according to operational regions before the alliance. Nissan North America had one set of rules; Nissan Europe another. Japan was a different story altogether. Getting these regions together under one set of standards (remaining sensitive to regional pay structures, of course) in such a short time was a monumental task.

The new structure introduced through the NRP created a global human resource department in Tokyo that works with regional committees in the different operational areas of the world. Just getting initial buy-in from the human resource staff in Tokyo was a challenge in the beginning, and implementing the new schemes, particularly in Japan, took longer than most NRP aspects because so many people "had to change their attitude" and ways of thinking before change could occur.

HUMAN RESOURCE CHANGES IMPLEMENTED UNDER NRP:

- Seniority was eliminated as a means of company advancement.
- Senior executive positions found to be redundant in the global structure were consolidated.
- Compensation schemes were revamped to reflect higher pay based on strong performance.
- Bonus pay was tied to the NRP's success for all employees.
- Frivolous expense accounts were eliminated.

Promoting employees with less seniority than others caused some minor problems internally. Nissan, like other Japanese companies, previously paid its employees based on tenure and age, fostering the "job for life" concept that rewarded longevity.

The longer an employee stayed at Nissan, the more money and more power they were given—regardless of performance. Typically, senior managers worked less, leaving tasks and long days at the office to the salary men while they enjoyed a more leisurely pace with lavish expense accounts, often treating associates to dinner, drinks, and other Japanese executive business customs.

Under the NRP senior executive positions found to be redundant in the global structure were consolidated, giving top level "advisers," who had few responsibilities and were accountable for nothing, new assignments within the company. The "advisers" or "coordinators" are familiar figures in Japanese companies with foreign subsidiaries. The positions were originally created so the foreign subsidiaries would have a consultant to ensure that Japanese management practices were carried out properly. After a number of years foreign subsidiaries were familiar with the Japanese way and the advisers had little to do. Ghosn changed that, assigning Nissan's advisers to positions with direct responsibilities.

Ghosn also consolidated twenty-nine product project Directors who reported to the product planning group into six program groups, headed by one program director. The new program directors are coordinated by Pelata and report directly to him and Ghosn. Known as "the six soldiers of Mr. Ghosn," the program directors became the backbone of Nissan's product line, with ultimate responsibility for the development, sales, and profitability of a model.

The regional operations groups, which gave up direct treasury and purchasing powers under the NRP, also saw the elimination of president positions when management was restructured.

The objective was to create a headquarters function in Tokyo, and keeping regional presidents made no sense under the new scheme, so they were eliminated operationally, creating clear management lines running from top levels in Tokyo (CEO and president and executive vice presidents) to North America, Europe, and general overseas markets, where regional positions at the highest levels are filled by senior vice presidents. The result: All executives have responsibilities and the chain of command is clear.

"Ghosn has made the management structure very simple and streamlined," Connelly says. "It's a very flat and very clean structure that makes responsibilities clear."

The lavish expense account perks were eliminated and Ghosn gave the companywide directive that all promotions and bonus pay at Nissan would be performance-based. He thought it only made sense for a car company—selling consumers performance-based products—to build reward and incentives systems around actual performance.

Although Ghosn's nominations for top positions, to date, have been veteran managers with years of verifiable results, they have not always had the most seniority, causing motivational problems for a few managers when older employees under them did not easily accept leadership from someone younger. Still, Ghosn ditched the seniority rule, believing tensions would ease as time eroded tradition.

Nissan now gives its key executives warrant bonds and incentive pay based on good performance—something not usually done in Japan. Strong performers were rewarded only with annual pay raises slightly higher than those given to poor performers—providing very little incentive for managers within the company to create change and push other employees around them to deliver better results. Top performers at Nissan today can get cash bonuses totaling 25 percent of their annual pay. The key, though, is that they must perform, because with the incentives came more individual responsibility and accountability, eliminating the potential for pointing fingers at others when problems arise. Word was sent throughout the company that those who performed would be rewarded, regardless of tradition and other factors typically regarded in Japan.

"Nationality, age, gender . . . none of these matters at Nissan anymore," says Kuniyuki Watanabe, senior vice president in human resources. "Only performance [matters]."

The level of bonuses given is also tied to the overall performance of Nissan, eliminating rewards based solely on regional strengths. For example, managers working in Smyrna, Tennessee, will receive incentive pay at one level if goals are met and exceeded at their plant. But to receive full incentive pay, Nissan, as a global entity, must be profitable. It is just one more way Nissan worked to bind its world operations together through common goals.

"It only makes sense to take a global view," Long says.

The link changed the mind-set of employees immediately, a Smyrna engineering manager said. Nissan North America employees who used to feel isolated from Japan are now interested in what happens with the company as a whole. "Everyone in Smyrna used to be mostly concerned with our goals and numbers," he says. "Maybe they would check the company's stock price every now and then. Now, they are paying a lot more attention to what is coming out of Tokyo."

Closing Plants

The most painful NRP element to implement, from an emotional standpoint in Japan, was undoubtedly the closing of plants and elimination of jobs in Nissan's home country. Nissan had more than 148,000 employees worldwide in 1999 before the NRP, with more than a third of those in Japan where market share had been declining since the mid-1970s. And although it's true that these plants manufactured many exported vehicles, like the Maxima and Pathfinder, which are sold in the United States, Nissan was barely operating at 50 percent capacity at plants in Japan, and domestic contraction was the answer. By reducing headcount by 21,000, or 14 percent of the total workforce, overall productivity ratios would increase more than 20 percent.

Laying off employees isn't readily accepted in Japan and manufacturing job reductions are more severe there than in most other countries because job opportunities are limited for midcareer workers no longer in the job-for-life scheme. In an effort to handle the plant closings "as smoothly as possible," Nissan offered transfers to all direct and semidirect employees at the plants that were to be closed. The job reductions were achieved by natural attrition; early retirement offered to eligible employees; and hiring at other plants that was "strictly limited" so openings could be filled by transferring employees.

Employees who were not laid off shared the pain of those who lost jobs, but they themselves did not suffer in the workplace since this wasn't a rank and file, penny-pinching conservation plan that forced company departments to use less paper and turn up the thermostat.

New Opportunities

The NRP was not all about job elimination, either. The plan actually created some jobs. Management had the courage and savvy to increase research and development investment while cost-cutting measures occurred in other areas so Nissan could build for the future.

The increased R&D emphasis called for more than 500 new jobs, most in Japan, and the new plant in Mississippi began hiring the first of its 4,000 employees not too long after construction began. The stress, though, was in Japan, where long-time employees had to make difficult choices, like whether to move or leave the company.

"As for the whole picture of Nissan, it wasn't so bad," Watanabe says. "But person to person, particularly in Japan, it was very difficult."

Nissan's challenge was no different than any manufacturer that sells products directly to consumers: keep the buying public happy. Many of the employees who took early retirement or found other jobs were life-long Nissan supporters who always bought Nissan products. Japan may have 125 million residents, but the company that had lost market share for a quarter of a century at home did not want to lose more good customers over past struggles.

"We try to take care of each person carefully," Watanabe says. "If they respect the company, they can still be a good Nissan customer."

Ghosn and others from Renault were struck by the "*gaman*"—or Japanese work ethic and job commitment—displayed by manufacturing employees until the very last vehicles rolled off the line at the closing plants. Not one vehicle was lost to interrupted production and plants closed without incident, a testament to the Japanese people.

"When Renault closed its Belgium plant it created a stir all over Europe," Klein says. "In Japan, we closed five plants in two years and there was no trouble, no big negative comments. They obviously were not happy about it, but we did not lose a single car. They worked hard until the very end, loyal to the company."

Klein attributes the smooth plant closings to the high level of discipline among Japanese workers and the continual flow of information given to employees about the changes that were occurring. "We explained in detail how this plan was important to the survival of the company," he says. "We gave them facts and figures with a lot of information."

Changing People

Though Nissan cut jobs and restructured management during the NRP, no management-level house cleaning occurred when Ghosn took command in 1999.

There were changes, certainly. Most notably, top-level positions were created for Pelata and Moulonguet. These positions were new and necessary to implement enhanced product planning and development; the more complex human resource and communication functions; and cross-company facilitation between Nissan and Renault.

The "adviser" positions were eliminated, forcing several

longtime executives to accept positions with more direct responsibility. Some left on their own, choosing retirement over revival. But Nissan's management cast, albeit reshuffled, is basically the same as it was before Ghosn arrived, taking into consideration the new, French faces.

Says Ghosn: "It is easy to change persons. It is much more difficult to change people."

The easiest thing to do during a management shift is to clean house, sending away nonsupporters and those who do not wholeheartedly support new ideas and tactics at the top. But Ghosn operates by a different philosophy. More than a few managers greeted his efforts with a tepid nature, and several executives voiced support during committee meetings with "negative" yes votes. That is, they raised their hand in support, but only halfheartedly, showing they were not completely behind the measures Ghosn proposed. Still, Ghosn wanted to give them time to change instead of starting over, and used an arsenal of factual information and results to win them over.

"It is more long-lasting and beneficial—more powerful— to change people than to change persons," he says.

Ghosn believes the experience and knowledge gained through years of service by veteran employees is worth more to a corporate leader and a company than an employee with less experience. Therefore, he tries to make personnel changes only when the people refuse to change after a reasonable period of time. In the interim, Ghosn considers changing the people a personal challenge that is actually an enjoyable part of management. The style is in keeping with his ultracompetitive nature. Simply casting off those who do not agree with him would be too easy.

"I do it, but only when necessary," he says. "I consider it a waste. It is more of a challenge to me to change people from within."

Aides say Ghosn only made one "fundamental" personnel change in his first three years on the job at Nissan and revel in the entirely new face they say emerged on the management team as implementation began to hit full stride, with disbelievers and dissenters numbering fewer with every passing day. It is impossible to please them all, of course. Reward for results has increased, but so has responsibility, forcing longtime employees to work harder than ever before. Internal polling shows that although some are not yet comfortable with the extra heat, they at least know the measures being taken are the right ones.

"I don't know if top executives and managers are all pleased, but I do know from internal responses they are more confident in the company and the job that is being done," Klein says.

Ghosn Named CEO

Ghosn was given a title promotion shortly after the first-year NRP results were announced, becoming Nissan's president and CEO. He had been given the title of chief operating officer when he was hired in 1999 and Hanawa officially maintained his position as president, though Ghosn called the shots.

What title Ghosn was to be given was a topic of much debate by Nissan's executive committee before he started work in the summer of 1999. The Japanese didn't want it to look like the foreign company that was coming to the rescue had total control, so the titles of president and CEO were reserved for a time when results showed they were deserved.

Ghosn was named Nissan's president in the summer of 2000, after the company successfully launched the NRP and was beginning to show positive results from its efforts. He was formally given the title of president and chief executive officer in the summer of 2001 in recognition of the company's strong numbers during the first full year of its revival plan.

Hanawa became chairman of the board, officially leaving no doubts as to who was in charge: President and CEO Carlos Ghosn, the man who had a vision that Nissan could be strong again and expand its presence globally with a unified, innovative brand.

The timing of the title promotions was poetic in a way because it followed the fast track of Ghosn's development as a world business leader. When he arrived he was without a doubt a seasoned turnaround expert who had led large operational divisions and managed thousands of employees. But he had not stood alone before in the limelight of corporate center stage, and perhaps no industry is as high profile in the United States, Europe, and Japan as the automotive industry.

Ghosn arrived in Japan as an operational leader and reformer, in title and reputation. But he listened and observed in an approachable and nonimposing manner and taught, motivated, and led employees in ways they had never seen before. His persona grew each step along the way of his first three months on the job and during the implementation of the NRP, and the public began to know Carlos Ghosn, president and CEO instead of Ghosn the operations leader.

A Language for All

The NRP announcement was the dawning of a new day in open communication for Nissan. It also was the moment in which employees from different cultures had to start working together in new ways to implement the aggressive measures.

Russia relied on glasnost for exposure to the world. Nissan relied on Ghosn, its multicultural leader who does not believe people have to speak the same language to communicate effectively.

The challenge: basic communication among some was difficult, to say the least. So difficult, in fact, that anyone studying the revival of Nissan and looking for reasons that the turnaround is more dramatic and unique than other corporate efforts can stop right here.

Multicultural companies certainly exist all over the world, but rare is the moment a whole team of top-level managers arrive from another country and in one day begin retooling the company and the minds of the people with a plan as massive as the NRP and a leader as different as Ghosn.

And most global unions do not involve backgrounds as different as French and Japanese.

The French expats and the few Americans who moved to Tokyo after the alliance were so perplexed by Japan and its hieroglyphic language that they were deep into solving the company's complex problems before they had learned to read and understand their mail. Every few days they would bring it to the office and gather Japanese friends to interpret bills from junk.

Two countries—two companies—could not have been more different when it came to communication. One is very verbal, open, and philosophical; the other is closely guarded and evasive, particularly when outsiders are involved, creating gaps that occurred for reasons other than the mere fact that French and Japanese are different languages.

The communication methods and habits within the cultures are so different that even when the same language is used, different understandings can result. For instance, Japanese businessmen often say "yes" repeatedly when being told something. It is a sign that they understand the dialogue and are absorbing it, not that they approve of what is being said. Imagine the potential for confusion.

French: "We think we need to close a plant."

Japanese: "Yes."

French: "Jobs will be lost."

Japanese: "Yes."

French: "We have no choice. It must be done."

Japanese: "Yes."

The conversation ends. The French are moving on, making plans to close a plant. The Japanese are only ready to begin considering it, having said "yes" simply as conversational confirmation that they understood what was being said.

Confusion never occurred at this magnitude, but cultural communication differences made for some interesting moments during high-level meetings and discussions. Speed was important and to-the-letter accuracy was crucial.

The communication issue was solved for the cross-company teams that were working together before the alliance was signed by skilled interpreters who massaged dialogue between the French and Japanese. The cross-functional teams were composed of mostly Japanese and used interpreters when necessary. But implementation of the NRP occurred office to office, person to person on a daily basis. Direction had to come from the highest levels of the company, which included the Renault expats manning new, key management positions in Tokyo offices staffed mostly by Japanese. Simple conversations were a challenge.

Executives and managers tell story after story of long meetings that should have been short, extended by language barriers. Viadieu, the only French expat in manufacturing in Tokyo—"they didn't need any help in that area"—said working everyday in a department composed totally of Japanese, him being the one exception, was difficult in the beginning, when not one person spoke the other's language. And it is not like they were discussing weekend plans. This was corporate turnaround, manufacturing reform at a fast-paced clip . . . hundreds of schemes, thousands of parts . . . the potential for one big-time headache.

"A meeting that should have lasted two hours took all day," he says, wiping his brow in mock distress while laughing at the memory. "It was not easy, but we had no choice. The risk of misunderstanding was very high, so we had to make sure. What I do know, is that by the end of the day, I was exhausted."

Viadieu remembers giving presentation slides to an assistant for translation to use in a meeting. The worker ran the presentation Viadieu had written in French through a computer translation program and returned it in English, supposedly ready for action. The translation was poor and the presentation was useless, but the assistant never knew.

"They had no idea it was wrong," he says. "But it was just words . . . it meant nothing."

He tells the story and others like it affectionately, emphasizing that he has since learned Japanese, while many of his fellow workers have learned English, believing that the struggle was good, forcing them to facilitate and get to know one another in different ways. Now he speaks a combination of French, Japanese, and English—every day.

Viadieu also talks about the Japanese people he works with and others in Tokyo he has met with unwavering and outspoken passion, saying the union between the corporations has given him a binational Ghosn-like view of the world. He says the Japanese, though typically more reserved in interpersonal communications than Westerners, are the most sincere and caring friends from the perspective of an entire culture one could find. They've turned initial language difficulties they faced at the office into language role reversal.

"We mix it up," he says. "It's kind of a game with my Japanese coworkers. They speak English and I speak Japanese."

Ghosn believes language differences should not be a hindrance to good business and that solutions can always be found when it comes to communication. After all, he became the leader of a Japanese company when he could not speak the language and implemented a multitude of changes in a very short time.

The solution: English became the official business language of Nissan in an effort to solve the communication problem, a drastic move at Tokyo headquarters considering that before the alliance almost all Nissan Japan employees were Japanese. Yes, English is taught in the schools. But textbook English is different than truly knowing the language conversationally. Breaking up Nissan's keiretsu may have grabbed international headlines, but enforcing English as the official "business language" of a major Japanese company might have been a bigger undertaking.

And Ghosn went a step farther, sending a direct message to executives and managers that learning English was important and those who mastered it would have a distinct advancement advantage within the company in the future. Many have responded, including some veteran executives who previously had very limited English vocabularies. The result is that most top-level meetings are now conducted in English.

The trick is to understand that Japanese people communicate differently in English than they do in their native language. Japanese tend to speak in an indirect manner when communicating with others, lacing requests with courteous, nonfrank dialogue. When they use English and know only certain, direct words conversations take on an entirely different manner.

"It can be brutal," Viadieu says. "They say, 'Give it to me.' In Japanese, they would say 'Please do so."

Ghosn, who knows several languages but only some Japanese, conducts most speeches in English and top Japanese executives use English when needed, even though they may not be totally comfortable or confident—an effort to show support for necessary corporate change. "Sometimes [using English] is painful for me, but I know it is the way for us to communicate even though there is less understanding on both sides," Watanabe says.

Still, there have been problems. Watanabe remembers a meeting attended by French and Japanese where one topic was thoroughly discussed for two hours—in English. At the end, he had to ask for explanations, having missed the meaning of many words. "French-English understanding is different than Japanese-English understanding."

Ghosn's solution: a company dictionary, containing forty key terms—in English.

Speaking Clearly

Because the implementation of the NRP was so involved and precise, and because automotive manufacturing is so precise in general, Nissan could not afford for misunderstanding to come from its Japanese-French-English dialogue. The dictionary gave clear meanings for necessary words used by management so that when they were used in meetings everyone would clearly know what meaning was intended. Employees at all levels, particularly those in Tokyo, were told to refer to the dictionary at all times so there was no confusion over what was being said.

"For example, the meaning of 'commitment' can be extremely variable," Ghosn said. "We created and shared the definition throughout the organization, so everybody understands the same thing."

The result of Nissan's cultural infusion is a picture of the

Japanese company that today looks something like a language pyramid at its headquarters facilities in Tokyo. Bottom floors are still staffed mostly by Japanese workers who typically speak Japanese with each other during the workday. But the higher one climbs, in terms of the physical structure of the building and the management structure of the company, the more English and French one hears. At the very top, the result is often a vegetable soup blend, where complete sentences from some executives contain multiple language components.

The irony is that communication in the management levels of Nissan, though it now comes in different forms, has never been clearer. Managers and executives have learned an entirely new style of "focus" communication in which they key on a few specific, direct words they all understand.

The result is a clear and understandable dialogue that is a major reason implementation of the NRP occurred so swiftly and effectively. It is a minor miracle, really, considering that some key employees could barely communicate when cross-functional teams were formed to formulate the NRP.

By the end of the first year, everyone at the company knew what these words meant: record profits.

CHAPTER SEVEN

There Are No Problems Good Products Can't Solve

Nissan tackled objectives of its revival plan so aggressively that all official commitments were reached and overachieved one full year ahead of schedule, prompting Ghosn to announce to the world in May 2002 that the three-year NRP was over in just two years.

The company posted its best-ever full year earnings in fiscal year 2001 and launched the first of several hot-selling, post-revival-plan vehicles that had it poised to enter another phase in the effort to turn around Nissan. Sales in Japan also rose incrementally, stopping the more than quarter century domestic erosion.

"Last year I told you Nissan was back," Ghosn said. "This year I will tell you that Nissan moved decisively toward establishing itself as a world-class, competitive, and profitable global auto company."

Ghosn used the announcement that the NRP was ending early as a springboard to the second half of Nissan's turnaround effort: NISSAN 180, a plan designed to focus on creating lasting profitable growth for the company. The new plan took effect April 1, 2002, or the beginning of Nissan's 2002 fiscal year. Its aim is to take Nissan from an automaker operating on a par level with competitors to the best in the world.

Ghosn is sitting in his executive office on the fifteenth floor of one of Nissan's two Tokyo headquarters buildings shortly after the company ended its record-setting 2001 performance, reflecting on a whirlwind year that without a doubt was the most remarkable in the company's history considering the range of advancements made in terms of financial and product advancement and public awareness. He says the work that was done by employees all over the world, overcoming obstacles ranging from cultural differences to short time frames given to achieve lofty goals, was unified and focused, giving off a global glow that reflected strongly on an emerging brand identity.

Nissan is no longer an ailing company losing money with invisible leadership and subpar cars to sell. It is a highly profitable company selling innovative products to eager consumers, under the direction of a charismatic leader grabbing headlines in major news publications all over the world. The company made money in 2000 and regained the confidence of employees. In 2001, Nissan made money *and* sold exciting products once again.

And that, says Ghosn, made all the difference.

There are no problems at a car company good products can't solve.

Ghosn has talked about products being the key to Nissan's lasting invigoration since the first months of his arrival. The automotive industry is built upon the foundation that consumers are romanced by cars in the largest, most profitable markets like the United States, Europe, and Japan. Exciting products that meet high customer demand will make even the stickiest of domestic human resource problems seem small by creating more jobs, more employee reward, and more internal gratification and corporate pride.

New Products Grab Headlines

That's exactly why Ghosn sent a headhunter to entice Shiro Nakamura to leave Isuzu and join Nissan as its head designer in 1999. Nissan needed new and it needed exciting.

Nakamura joined Nissan just as the NRP was being announced, tackling the company's aggressive plans to launch twenty-two new models in less than three years, a pace not imaginable before the alliance. He and his team of designers worked frenetically at the company's design and technical center, located an hour and a half outside of Tokyo, trying to meet the objectives of working fast and delivering results good enough to transform one of the world's largest automakers.

"I have twelve or more meetings every day and I rarely work fewer than fourteen hours," says Nakamura, a twenty-eight-year veteran of the auto industry. "The pace we are working is amazing. It's an unbelievable amount of work, but I don't think about it because this does not feel like work. This is an opportunity."

"This" is a license from Carlos Ghosn to create out of the box automobile designs with "Japanese DNA" that comes with the demand that it happen at a breakneck pace rarely, if ever, seen before in the industry.

Outdated design was a big part of Nissan's problems when Ghosn arrived.

Invigorated design would be the heart of its revival.

Nakamura jumped to Nissan from his heralded position at Isuzu despite initial fear that Nissan would face complications from the union of French and Japanese companies. He was also concerned about the lack of creativity that was shown at Nissan in the past and the general perception that the company was stale and dated. The deciding factor: full-scale commitment to product revitalization.

"Ghosn convinced me that he wanted to use design as an important driving force of Nissan," says Nakamura, who was given creative authority over company engineers.

Nakamura's first job was to rekindle relationships between Nissan's design centers in Europe, Japan, and the United States. Design at Nissan had been fragmented by regions before the alliance, just like almost every other aspect of the company. But there was a difference. Design was fragmented because head designers in Tokyo ruled. Nissan's North American design studio, run by Hirshberg as Nissan Design International, functioned as a satellite office. NDI was isolated except when directives were given, causing friction and a competitive atmosphere between design groups. Everything had to be sent to Japan for approval, and to say a team concept was lacking is putting it mildly.

A story is told within the company about a U.S.-designed, second-generation Infiniti Q45 that was scrapped by orders from Tokyo in favor of a clone of the Japan-market Cima so that it could sit on a less expensive platform. The result was a mediocre model with a smaller engine that American buyers shunned. Designers had no say-so with engineers and decisions were made during production that totally changed design intent.

Some strong products emerged from the U.S. Design Center out of sheer strength, including the Pathfinder, Infiniti J30, and Xterra. The problem was that the best vehicles had no central theme with other Nissan products. The Maxima, for example, was one of Nissan's most successful cars. It was designed in America and approved in Japan, developing a solid base of loyal customers that still exists. But the car matched nothing in Nissan's worldwide lineup, creating a jolt to the notion of brand loyalty. Customers liked the Maxima but did not care what company designed and built it because they could not identify with other Nissan products that were drastically different.

Enter Ghosn, Pelata, Nakamura, Tom Semple, and others who immediately identified Nissan's lack of global recognition in the vehicles it produces and did something about it. The first step was reopening lines of communication between Tokyo, Nissan Design America, and Nissan Design Europe, in Munich, Germany. No more dictatorship and no more regional isolation. The top levels of design teams began working together to strategize and find common threads that could be used in design throughout the world. Semple, who took over for Hirshberg at the time of the alliance and restructured Nissan Design America, says the quest to identifying elements that can be used globally has been an ongoing process but that progress is being made through open lines of communication and product evolution.

The secret lies in global collaboration, beginning in the preproduction and preparatory stages of design. Semple says the story of the creation of the new Z car is a perfect example of how designers in Japan, the United States, and Europe can work together to jointly develop a car.

The U.S. version of the Z car went out of production in 1996 due to emission control issues, and it was too expensive—the 1996 300ZX convertible had a manufacturer's suggested retail price of $45,999—by then to attract the same type of buyers who flocked to the old Z car years before. The original 240Z was a $3,500 phenomenon, blending European styling with Japanese engineering and reliability. When Nissan was struggling in the late 1990s, before the alliance, U.S. designers began seriously toying with designs of an all-new Z car that could be produced for America and hopefully reverse the company's fortunes.

The project was just done on the side in the United States, since designers had no official authorization from Tokyo. Still, they worked to develop a car design that embodied the performance and value of the old 240Z but contained a hint of visual appeal reminiscent of the 300ZX that was sold in Japan after it was no longer produced for the United States market. Models were shown at the 1999 auto show in Detroit and the energy level the car created prompted the project to be officially incorporated into Nissan's strategic plan.

The alliance was formed and along came Ghosn, who immediately gave full, enthusiastic endorsement to the Z project. Once the NRP was announced and Nissan's global design effort came to life, the latest Z car became the standard-bearer for company designers in collaboration and joint development. Designs from Nissan Design America were selected after initial work among the Europe, Japan, and U.S. teams. Design development was then transferred to Nakamura and Japan, where adjustments were made, but the original concept from NDA remained intact.

The result was a globally designed, 287-horsepower sports car that created excitement where before there was frustration from Nissan designers who were regionally isolated but were now speaking through products with one voice. The latest Z is one of many cars on the way that was created to be buyer-specific in a framework of innovative, Japanese style. It is a market-sensitive, global design approach to lineup invigoration that Ghosn is betting Nissan's future on.

Nakamura, if anything, has infused more Japanese "DNA" into Nissan's lineup despite the fact that all U.S. designs had to be approved in Japan before the alliance. Because there was previously little cross-work in design, Japan functioned in more of a dictator role for American designers. Nakamura wants all Nissan products to contain the best of innovative Japanese design concepts while integrating the best from North America and Europe, so the products are distinctively Nissan and reflective of the company's multicultural and global ways of thinking and working.

"Still, when I travel to the United States and Europe I ask for comments from people about what they think about U.S. model cars," says Nakamura, who was named to the 2002 *Automotive News* All Stars for design. "I listen to comments and try to make the best decisions so we meet [regional] desires with a global product."

One example: the full-size truck, a "very American domestic product" that will look nothing like products currently on the market from the U.S. Big Three. Nakamura,

Semple, and company are giving it their own "taste of innovation," blending American and Japanese styles. The result is a fully functional, full-size truck that looks and feels like a Japanese sports car. The product is so different there is actually nothing like it on the U.S. market today, giving Nissan a much-needed opportunity to find new markets.

Nissan had just started to benefit from its new global design approach at the end of 2001 when the first completely post-NRP vehicles hit showrooms. The all-new Nissan Altima and Infiniti G35 sedan sold in record numbers and received rave reviews in North America, while the restyled March was the hottest new car in Japan, giving the company a legitimate chance of regaining long-lost market share in its home country.

The subcompact March is an updated version of a ten-year-old design. Nissan pioneered the subcompact market in Japan in 1992 with the release of the March, but waited too long to update the model, giving Honda and Toyota, Nissan's domestic rivals, the head start in a new version of the subcompact category, one in which Japanese consumers want cars that are small and affordable but fun to drive and uniquely styled. Honda's Fit ($8,100 base model) and Toyota's Vitz ($5,385 base model) sold thousands of units and created a buzz all over the country when each debuted before the restyled March. Nissan was working on plans for an updated March, certainly, before Ghosn and company arrived, but the ultimate product, the one creating such a stir in Japan in spring 2002, was the result of more than a few tweaks by new management.

The March comes in head-turning new colors, including paprika orange and lima bean green—food ingredient colors. It has on-board e-mail and navigational systems typically reserved for luxury models, side airbags, and a stronger engine. The basic unit is priced below $8,000.

Early indications are that Nissan has found a winner. The company announced in March 2002 that it had received 25,000 orders for the car the first week it was offered for sale, and by the end of April there were 55,000 orders. In comparison, Honda received 23,000 orders for the Fit during the first ten days it was on the market in Japan in 2001, and Toyota had 20,000 orders for the Vitz when it debuted in 1999, giving the March a victory in initial customer demand. More important, the March is giving Nissan a legitimate chance to achieve measurable domestic market share growth for the first time in twenty-seven years by creating new and younger Nissan customers.

"The capacity of a car to attract buyers to your brand is what makes the difference between a good product and a hit," Ghosn said. "Today, forty percent of March buyers are coming to us from another brand. We believe this is an extremely positive sign of the significant contribution we expect from this vehicle to our overall performance in Japan."

Nissan's Car of the Year

The frenzy over the March is no different than what Nissan is experiencing at the same moment in the United States, easily Nissan's most profitable market, as postalliance and NRP models of the Nissan Altima and Infiniti G35 sedan are selling so fast dealers literally can't keep them on lots.

The Altima, produced in the United States at Nissan's Smyrna, Tennessee, plant, is a model that got lost in time, much like the March. Its overdue revamp was more than a face-lift as well. The Altima got more power, more room, and as one reviewer said, "some Z-car essence." Nissan's big boost came in January 2002 in Detroit when a panel of forty-nine writers who gather annually at the North American International Auto Show to determine the best products the industry has to offer deemed the all-new Altima North American Car of the Year. The Altima, interestingly, was the first car model by a Japanese manufacturer to ever receive this award. Nissan's original line capacity in Smyrna for the Altima is 200,000 units per year; yet, due to its popularity, the company hopes to squeeze in an additional 20,000 to meet demand.

"What's happening with the Altima is incredible," says Jed Connelly, who as senior vice president of sales and marketing for Nissan North America is the company's highest-ranking sales official in the United States. "It's the first major car to come out after the Renault-Nissan alliance and it's a classic example [of changes] at Nissan. This kind of attention is something we are going to get used to."

The Infiniti G35 sedan, the first of four new products scheduled for Infiniti in the 2002 fiscal year, debuted with similar fanfare. A caption in the May 2002 edition of *Men's Journal* dubbed the G35 "the coolest Japanese machine since Nintendo." Accompanying text gave similar praise: "Considering Infiniti's struggles, it's safe to say that stakes for the G35 are higher than Woody Harrelson. Not to worry. Similar in looks and specifications to the Audi A4 3.0 and Mercedes-Benz C320, the G35 has a big V-6, rear-wheel drive, and powerful yet understated styling."

The G35 went on sale in March 2002, helping to lead Infiniti, Nissan North America's luxury division, to its best sales month in history in March and again in April. Infiniti reported March sales of 8,628 units, a 7.4 percent increase versus March of the previous year. Infiniti sales increased 60 percent in April over the previous year.

It's the first time in years such praise has been heaped upon Nissan's products. It is also the first time since Ghosn and his team of French expats arrived from Renault that the media is talking about cars, not problems. But getting Nakamura to claim victory on the moment of product invigoration might be impossible.

"We are not yet successful," he says, noting that Nissan still has more than twenty new models to launch in the next three years, including the full-size truck. "It is too early to relax . . . I can just say that I am at least not disappointed with results so far."

Nakamura is, however, surprised at the speed with which Nissan climbed out of its catatonic state. "Yes," he says, drawing the word out for effect, "amazing, really. It has been much faster than I anticipated. Maybe faster than anyone anticipated."

Numbers Speak Louder

The same can be said for Nissan's financial results. The Nissan Revival Plan was supposed to take three years to complete, yet Ghosn announced at the annual Nissan supplier meeting held in Tokyo in February 2002 that it would be concluded on March 31, 2002, the official end of the company's 2001 fiscal year. The plan that many said could not be implemented in any amount of time was concluded in just two years as Nissan's key NRP targets—achieving profitability the first year; achieving an operating margin of at least 4.5 percent; and halving net consolidated automotive debt to less than 700 billion yen ($10 billion)—were met and, in most cases, handily surpassed, one full year ahead of schedule.

Precisely, Nissan's consolidated operating profits for fiscal year 2001 (ending March 31, 2002) were $3.92 billion, resulting in an operating margin of 7.9 percent of net sales, the highest in the company's history. Nissan's automotive debt at the end of 2001 was just $3.48 billion, well below the NRP commitment. Sales figures were stagnant, actually declining 1.4 percent from 2000, but most of the decline was in the first half of the year as the company gained significant momentum from the new products at the end of the year. Still, the bottom line was anything but stagnant: Nissan's 1999 net profit was a $5.7 billion loss; Nissan's 2001 net profit was $2.98 billion.

Nissan's stock price rose on the news that the company had posted its second straight year of record profits. Shares hit a fifty-two-week high ($15.97 per share on the NASDAQ) the day the announcement was made, culminating a year in which Nissan's stock price doubled despite weak financial markets in America and Japan.

Just two years before Nissan was flirting with disaster, posting a net income loss of 684 billion yen and showing long-term debts on the books totaling more than 2.5 trillion yen. Now, it was raising shareholder dividends (from seven to eight yen per share) and announcing its best net income results in the company's seventy-year history.

"The Nissan Revival Plan is over," Ghosn said when publicly announcing the company's 2001 financial results in Tokyo in May 2002. "[The record results] are the fruit of the NRP, fruit that even the most optimistic of outside observers in 1999 didn't think of."

Ghosn said Nissan's 120,000-plus worldwide employees deserved credit for believing change could occur despite previous failed revival efforts at the company. He said people who wondered why he looked for answers within the company could now see the benefits of that action. "When we arrived in 1999 morale was low. They were concerned the company might not survive. I traveled to Nissan facilities throughout the world and was immediately impressed by the workforce. I believed they could turn this company around. They did."

The achievement of record-setting profits was hardly a moment of exhilaration for Ghosn and other key Nissan executives, who saw the eye-catching results as more of a silver bullet piercing the level of skepticism that had enveloped Nissan and its revival plan effort than victory. Nissan might have been one of the top ten automakers in the world before, but it was operating far below its potential and future prospects were getting worse by the moment as competitors zoomed by. The NRP helped the company get back to a level playing field.

But Ghosn is a man who plays at business the same way he plays competitive bridge: to win. He is an engineering perfectionist who is not one to settle for second or third best. He believes setting sights too low is asking for structural flaws, making Nissan's metamorphosis, in his eyes, far from complete.

Even a momentary blink could derail three years of hard work.

"Be vigilant," he tells employees.

Taking Responsibility

Despite the success, Nissan had its problems in 2001. The company did only moderately well with models in Japan like the new Bluebird Sylphy sedan and X-Trail sport utility, which sold to expectation, while other recent lineup additions, like the Stagea wagon, midsize sedans Primera and Skyline, and the Cima, a renamed Infiniti Q45, sold below expectation. The economy in Japan was still an issue, which was why the inexpensive March and the Moco, Nissan's new minicar in the Japanese market, was selling better than other, more expensive restyled models.

Nissan did manage to end many years of market share decline, but Japan is being counted on for thousands of additional unit sales in future plans, and the company cannot afford to miss in its home country. Ghosn's solution: He took responsibility for the Japanese market himself, serving as the operations director for Nissan Japan—easily the company's biggest market challenge considering the year-after-year domestic sales decline. Why? Because Ghosn thinks the leader of a company should be directly responsible for the biggest problems.

"When we are out of the woods in Japan, I will leave [the

responsibility] to someone else," he says. "Right now it is the toughest challenge we have. It needs to be my responsibility."

Nissan was also plagued by competition and currency problems in Europe in 2001, eliminating most profit and stifling sales growth in the region. Still, the year was considered a moderate success for Nissan Europe because the company managed to post a small profit by stopping sales that were previously occurring for the sake of market share only. Europe was essentially the same story as Japan albeit on a smaller scale. Tepid results were victories due to the size of the challenge and considering that Nissan of old would have been clobbered in similar circumstances.

Overall, 2001 was the year in which the quick and strong results Ghosn was looking for when he came to Nissan two years before came together in full view, in terms of financial reform and product revival, reinforcing the strength of the alliance and reform efforts made in Japan.

The March is a symbol of Nissan's advancement because it isn't just a small car selling for less than eight grand that the public likes; it is the first Nissan product to share a platform with Renault, revealing a blend of Japanese design (Nakamura) and European style (Pelata) with a global stamp of approval (Ghosn). And Nissan's $3.92 billion in 2001 operating profits is not just another black corporate number on a line; it is a message to the Japanese business community that drastic measures, such as job cuts and keiretsu reform that go against time-honored traditions, created domestic change while enhancing global opportunity.

Drawing Attention

This combination of invigorated products and strong financial results drew attention to Nissan and Ghosn in 2001 and the first half of 2002 beyond anything the company or its leader had experienced before. Nissan's CEO was the subject of a Japanese comic book series—"The True Life of Carlos Ghosn"— that sold more than 500,000 copies of each issue, mostly to subway-riding businessmen eager to learn more about Nissan's CEO.

When Ghosn was contacted about doing the Japanese "manga" he was given the option of participating with the publisher or not, but told the series would be done regardless. He contacted another Japanese businessman who had recently been featured in one but had declined to work with the publisher. He told Ghosn he would do it differently next time if given a choice again since cooperation meant having a measure of control.

Ghosn, the leader who loves controlling communications, worked with the publisher and sat for more than twenty-four hours of interviews, giving new meaning to the hardworking "7–11" nickname he had earned the first year in Japan. Ghosn got to review story lines before they were published, and the comic series was a hit, giving Japanese businessmen biographical insight into the country's new superhero.

One issue portrays a young Ghosn sitting by a fence in the schoolyard with his eyes closed. A car drives by and the young Ghosn listens to the sound of the motor of an out-of-sight car on the other side of the fence.

"Cadillac Eldorado," he says.

"Bingo," says his friend.

• • •

Ghosn doesn't like talking about his celebrity status that has developed in Japan, preferring instead to focus on the company and its products. Yet, since becoming Nissan's leader, he has spent hours in interviews with journalists from around the world so they can learn about him, down to his childhood and personal life. He sat for twenty-four hours for one project and let another into his home, allowing a photographer to capture him at the breakfast table with his family in their Tokyo apartment. For Ghosn it is simply a matter of giving others the information they need to build trust in Nissan. His reasoning: The public image of a corporate leader is always reflected upon the company.

Ghosn's attention to public relations details has paid off. He was named by *Fortune* magazine as Asia's 2002 Businessman of the Year. He was also named "Industry Leader of the Year" and "Top CEO–Asia" by *Automotive News* in the United States in 2001, and received a repeat performance as "Top CEO–Asia" in 2002 from *Automotive News. BusinessWeek* named Ghosn one of the "Top 25 Managers of the Year" in 2001; he was ranked number one in *Time*/CNN's "25 Most Influential Global Business Executives" in 2001; was named "Executive of the Year" by *American Industries* magazine in 2002; and named "Man of the Year" in 2002 by *Automobile* magazine.

The list for Carlos Ghosn goes on: a best-selling book in Japan; a first-person feature in the *Harvard Business Review;* feature stories in the likes of the *Wall Street Journal* and *BusinessWeek;* selection as Man of the Year by *Le Journal de l' Automobile* of France.

Ghosn has caught on so in trendy Japan that he takes his

children to Disneyworld Tokyo and a swarm of people follow around the corporate hero, whispers of "Ghosn-san" filling the air. He interviews on Japanese television and a housewife gets weak-kneed over his talk of reform.

An element the Japanese like about Ghosn is that he is a family man who seems to easily blend sixty-hour work weeks and an international schedule of meetings with fatherhood. At home on the weekend he avoids work—not even checking e-mails—and wears jeans around the house and spends quality time with his children so they can see Ghosn the father, not Ghosn the public CEO. The family can be seen together at events ranging from soccer games to sumo wrestling matches on the weekends—a refreshing sight for many Japanese who have felt a strain on the family amid clustered housing, long commutes, long working hours, expensive child-rearing costs, and a troubled economy.

A Japanese group that appreciates his attention to family gave Ghosn the honor he is most proud of: Best Father of the Year.

It is different in France and America, of course, where business leaders are not viewed with the same passion they are in Japan, but his style is recognized where it counts; in university halls and corporate boardrooms where new management practices are studied and copied. Ghosn's piece for the *Harvard Business Review* focused on his cross-company and cross-functional team approach to management, revealing ways he saved the business without losing the company.

The clippings and crooning are evidence that many outside of Nissan recognize something different is going on inside the company. They are also signs—take note of the geographic breadth from which the attention has come—

that change is occurring in more ways than one can detect from a dealer showroom or a corporate profit-and-loss statement.

Before the alliance, Nissan was a conservative, tightly held Japanese corporation with upper ranks closed to outsiders, or, to be more blunt, closed to anyone who wasn't a Japanese male with longtime service to the company. It was struggling to stay afloat and losing market share year after year. Three years after the alliance Nissan is building a new plant in predominantly black Canton, Mississippi; is owned in part by a French company; and is led by a CEO who has made it clear that promotions and filled vacancies at even the highest levels will go to the most productive and qualified, regardless of age, gender, or background.

"[Ghosn] sees all people the same," says Kuniyuki Watanabe, senior vice president in charge of human resources at Nissan. "All that matters to him is what they can contribute to Nissan."

International Fusion

This multicultural success—how a team of French executives, working with a team of seasoned Japanese executives and a sprinkling of strong-minded Americans, none speaking the same language—all under the guidance of a multicultural leader—found a way to work together and turn around an ailing company in a very short time with innovative products and fat profits are what make this turnaround story different from others.

Walk the halls of Nissan's corporate offices in Tokyo and quickly learn that even basic conversations among some employees can be a struggle, almost three years after the alliance. The best evidence of this idiomatic melting pot can seep out of the highest offices, where the dialogue of the moment is anyone's guess—English, French, Japanese. More typical is a mixture, blended in the most unexpected ways. Stick around long enough, though, and learn that good communication and clear vision is at the heart of Nissan's revival.

Few at the company are shy when it comes to identifying the catalyst of the simple and clear messages being passed. They point to Ghosn, the man who raises the bar after every step is made and sees the world as a place limited only by the perceptions and preconceived notions of others.

Launching a New Plan

This vision of greatness is why Ghosn keeps pushing Nissan and its people to higher ground despite record achievements along the way. Just as everyone was about to take a breath after furiously blitzing the NRP, Ghosn strategically used the announcement that Nissan was ending the plan one year early and had posted record-setting profits to launch the company's next strategic revival phase: NISSAN 180, a blueprint intended to create dramatic sales growth (one million more units sold by the end of fiscal year 2004 compared to fiscal year 2001), higher operating margin (8 percent), and zero net automotive debt, all within three years.

NISSAN 180 began in April 2002 with targets so aggressive that, if reached within three years, Nissan's total five-year turnaround effort under Ghosn and company—considering debt reduction, profit reform, and product growth—would be one of the most dramatic on record for an established company of its size. It is arguably far more aggressive than the NRP, yet almost nobody outside the company, publicly at least, is saying it cannot or will not happen after seeing two years of results after the alliance.

"Through NRP we transformed a struggling company into a good company; through NISSAN 180, we will transform a good company into a great company," Ghosn said. "The achievement of NISSAN 180 will rely on four pillars: more revenue, less cost, more quality and speed and a maximized alliance with Renault."

And it will rely on this: the ability of Carlos Ghosn to inspire the people to achieve the impossible once again.

CHAPTER EIGHT

Simplicity Comes from Hard Work

If you want to know exactly how Carlos Ghosn turned Nissan from a struggling company into a profitable one aiming to be among the best automotive manufacturers in the world you will not find all of the answers in the nuts and bolts management techniques used during the revival effort.

The turnaround began when Ghosn changed the minds of the people within the company. It started in Tokyo with the Japanese employees and spread to operational posts throughout the world. Longtime workers slow to change before began using new dialogues and processes in everyday work that they were not familiar with before Ghosn's arrival. They began thinking differently.

For the Japanese particularly, this was no small task considering Japan Inc. is based on tradition and the people do not accept change easily. Even small things that seem strange to

Westerners—like the way Japanese businessmen continually, incessantly, exchange business cards, or how an early ending to a scheduled meeting is offensive despite the fact that the work was completed—are upheld by young and old alike in Japan.

The country's broader business practices have been studied and revered inside the country and out since the 1970s and 1980s, when the likes of Nissan, Honda, and Toyota assaulted U.S. automakers with an onslaught of superior products. The Japanese way was so superior when it came to manufacturing and design that some of the largest companies in America even studied and tried to emulate the style. The Japanese themselves developed a superior attitude, and rightfully so. But when the economic bubble burst and times got tough the people stuck to old ways, and companies like Nissan paid the price. It took an outsider who approached the problems from the inside to get the people to respond and accept new ways of working. "The people are the same," Norio Matsumura says. "The difference is Carlos Ghosn. He restructured the mind of the people in the company."

He did it with a flair and familiarity uncommon for an outsider in Japan. From the first day he arrived, those around him learned, there's never a dull moment with Carlos Ghosn. He is a witty but impatient person who does nothing without a high level of calculation and intensity. When he speaks, he is typically direct and honest. If it's true, he's not afraid to say it. And he cannot help but lace his thoughts and comments with a philosophical style reflective of his French education and days spent rationalizing people and life with fellow students in Paris.

Ghosn is not a leader who wins people over by beating them into submission with his lofty position, throwing his CEO title at them in ways in which they cannot respond. Instead, he attacks with facts and conversational wit, leaving many would-be enemies on his side, or, at the very least, not willing to challenge him because of his never-ending arsenal. He is an energetic type who enjoys treating those around him to moments of frankness and revelation with constant reminders that life's challenges, be they business or social, are never as complex as they may seem. It is a style and skill Ghosn uses to persuade those around him to accept what previously seemed impossible and walk away from stern moments with the taskmaster with accepting, if not warm, feelings about him and their daunting job ahead. It's also a style and skill that was completely foreign in Japan and at Nissan before Ghosn arrived in 1999.

Three years later there is a different story to tell.

The demanding man at the top challenged the people by making them an integral part of the change and by showing them that new ways can work when old ones do not. And it worked. Managers and executives have adopted his leadership styles and techniques at such a high degree it is striking to an outside observer. Veteran executives—not an easily adaptable group in any company or culture—who have worked at Nissan for more than twenty years use terms like "commitment" and "target" and methods like transparency and cross-functional communication in everyday work that just three years before they had never been exposed to. The veteran employees may not always like what they are doing but they at least are doing it, evidence that they recognize Nissan's new ways are helping.

"These words weren't spoken here three years ago . . . they've easily adopted them," Klein says.

Executives and managers say this fact—that the new management style and way of thinking is so ingrained throughout the company—shows them that Nissan has changed for good and that Ghosn's way is now also Nissan's way. The style, in general, is a mixture of simplification, clarity, motivation, implementation, and expectation. Ghosn lays out the challenge to employees simply and clearly; he secures promises from them as to what they can deliver; employees focus on implementation, pushing for ground beyond commitment levels, and delivering to expectations beyond their promise.

Shiro Tomii, a senior vice president in Japan, sums Ghosn's style up this way:

- establishes high, yet achievable objectives
- makes clear to all roles and levels of responsibility
- works with speed
- checks on progress
- appraises results based on fact

Simple and Clear

The issues Nissan has faced in its turnaround efforts have been complex. There is nothing simple about the likes of a multicultural corporate alliance; keiretsu breakup; cross-company teams consisting of members who speak different languages; and automotive manufacturing, purchasing, and design schemes.

Yet clear, concise plans and instruction from the top is exactly what employees at Nissan repeatedly say is a key element in Nissan's revival. Ghosn takes personal pride in making the complex seem clear to those around him and searches during every meeting he attends for the point or points among masses of information that others are most likely to understand. The story goes that in troubleshooting meetings, when others are debating causes and possible solutions of a problem, Ghosn sits idly by, listening for input from others. Once a stalemate is reached, Ghosn, predictably, speaks up, having zeroed in on a seemingly simple yet finite point—the answer they've all been searching for but missed.

This ability to go straight to the problem or priority makes Ghosn an easy leader to follow. But Viadieu notes that he is anything but a simple man or manager. "He's easy and difficult at the same time." Translation: Ghosn speaks clearly and is easy to understand but his challenges and expectations of others are quite complex.

It's an analytical talent Ghosn has developed from his high level of engineering training, which he mixes with his understanding of how to work with people and explain solutions to them. Ghosn believes making issues simple and clear requires complex thinking—and hard work. But it is a leadership necessity in an international work environment where taking understanding for granted is a costly mistake.

"It's true, I have a lot of taste for things that are simple and clear and I have this in common with the Japanese people," Ghosn says. "A teacher once told me, it takes a lot of hard work to make something complex seem simple."

Ghosn once told a mathematics professor in college that he

didn't understand what he was saying in an explanation so "it must be wrong." The professor told Ghosn simplicity was a sign of "intelligence and hard work." It made an impression on Ghosn, who works so hard on clarity in all communications regarding Nissan it makes people around him sweat when speeches have to be made or presentations given. He has been known to spend hours debating a handful of sentences in a speech, believing that saying it exactly right is mandatory to communicating the message clearly, leaving no doubt among employees, shareholders, or consumers. He is in fact "picky" on all communications, external and internal, believing that every sentence—every word—must be completely understandable to all.

When asked why the CEO makes Nissan work so well, Klein says, "Simplicity. He has a real capability to make things simple. We were starting with a very complex situation and he was able to organize it into something very simple and he has communicated the message."

Instilling Motivation and Confidence

The struggling Japanese business economy and the inability to change caused a deep loss of confidence and motivation within Nissan, factors Ghosn considers essential to the success of a company. That's why one of his first assessments was that Nissan people needed to feel "a sense of urgency" about the company.

Previous reform efforts failed because Nissan employees

collectively were not motivated to change because they didn't have confidence that plans would work. The result was that some pieces were done; others were not. The plans were soon abandoned and confidence among employees sank even more.

Ghosn says instilling motivation is easy when you like what you do and believe in the cause. "You better like it, if you want to do well," he says. "You never succeed in anything without liking it and you never succeed in business without motivation."

The strategy was to allow the Japanese to resurrect the company by making them active participants in planning and implementing change. There was plenty of sweat and doubt in the beginning as many Japanese employees obliged with and worked with management because they "had no choice at the time." The motivating factor was Ghosn telling them to find ways to save the company. But CFTs began to click and brainstorm, giving management literally hundreds of ideas; and it was not long after the NRP was launched before the first positive quarterly results came in and internal confidence swelled within the company. Now they believed in Ghosn and the alliance and got additional motivation from new incentives and pride in their rising-stock company.

Listening

Saying that Ghosn believes listening is important to good leadership can create a "so what" reaction since many CEOs are adept at getting information from others with a keen ear. But with Ghosn, it isn't just a matter of him being a good listener; it's who he is listening to, which is anybody who has valid information to help Nissan and the Renault Nissan Alliance, no matter their rank in the company or society.

Ghosn quickly established this point during his initial days at Nissan when he toured plants, dealerships, and other company operations throughout the world, speaking with everyone, from employees working the floor to division presidents. It was a drastic change for Nissan, since in Japan executives are not typically seen fraternizing with entry-level employees, but for Ghosn it was a necessity to properly evaluate the company, a throwback to his days spent working the floor in his training days at Michelin.

In a personal conversation Ghosn waits until you completely finish a thought before responding, surprising given his general lack of patience. If you are in a heavy-hitting company strategy session, he values focused input—no vagueness—from anyone who believes he or she has a solution. But more important, he effectively pries information from those with whom he engages in conversation by using intuitive questioning, reflective of his French contemplative education.

If You Can't Listen, You Can't Command

It's a technique that ties directly into the "always start with a clean sheet of paper" concept where Ghosn arrives at new challenges and situations with no preconceived notions so people and issues can be seen on merit alone.

"You must give people a chance to say what they believe is the problem or the solution," he says. "Whether you follow it is a different story. By listening to people . . . you establish familiarity with them and automatically you shorten the distance. Suddenly, what you are talking about is not something so foreign to them."

Talking and listening to people helped Ghosn get rid of the initial "cost killer" image in Japan that had followed him from France. He sensed people at Nissan and in Japan thought he was coldhearted when he arrived but experience showed them otherwise. "Ghosn-san understood the solution to Nissan's problems was within the employees," says Katsumi Nakamura, a senior vice president. "He asked, 'What do we need to do?' He's very good at looking into the minds of the employees and hearing what they have to say."

Speed

Speed is a necessity when rescuing a struggling company, but Ghosn stresses that good leaders do not sacrifice prudence for the sake of quick action. In other words: Don't react fast; learn to work fast.

Ghosn's ability to handle multiple tasks is a personal quality that continues to turn the heads of those who are closest to him and have known him the longest. They say his speed in decision-making and emphasis on short deadlines helped push sluggish Nissan into warp speed in terms of action within the management ranks of the company. Issues that were previously studied for months, if not years, are now solved within weeks, if not days.

An example: Ghosn was present during a Nissan conceptual meeting about product "DNA" among Japanese and French participants shortly after taking over in 1999. Discussions were translated back and forth between Japanese and English, depending on who was speaking. The goal was to make headway in determining what qualities of the company and its Japanese heritage make Nissan products unique. After the meeting some Japanese participants expressed frustration over the format used, saying they needed training for such discussions. Ghosn wasn't sympathetic, telling the group he wanted a winning global brand strategy within months.

This happened routinely, employees innocently throwing up barriers that had little to do with the actual problems at hand because they were overwhelmed by new processes and ways of working. But Ghosn continued to demand quick but thorough decisions. He does the same himself, rarely mulling over even major issues long at all. He stresses, though, that all decisions at Nissan are made only after heavy consideration of facts. The difference is, he works hard at finding answers quickly and effectively, and tackles multiple tasks in a short period of time, leaving little, if anything, left undone.

"I never shoot from the hip on anything . . . I consider that to be arrogant and dangerous to the company," Ghosn says. "But it's true that I work quickly. I am able to handle multiple tasks in a short time because I work very hard at it."

Another example used to describe Ghosn's speed in decision-making involves the full-size pickup truck coming to market in the United States in 2003. Dealers and sales and marketing personnel had been telling executives in Tokyo for several years that Nissan needed a full-size truck. Nothing was ever done. Jed Connelly and Norio Matsumura took Ghosn to meet with a group of dealers while he was in his whirlwind fact-finding mission shortly after taking the job. What Ghosn heard overwhelmingly was that Nissan needed a full-size pickup truck to open paths to new customers in America.

The truck was officially on the drawing board in an instant and Nissan was looking for a site to build its second U.S. manufacturing plant. It decided on Canton, Mississippi, and three other potential sites in the southeast as four locations under consideration. A decision that quick in the large and often sluggish auto manufacturing industry is rare, but Ghosn says it was not made without all information on the table.

"I never make a decision without the facts," he said. "I take particular care not to make capricious decisions. By listening to people and observing, you build your own knowledge. If you don't have enough information, making a decision is a mistake. If you need to get more information, you have to make sure you get it and come back quickly with an answer, especially in a crisis."

Other examples of speed used in Nissan's turnaround effort are more obvious, like the fact that the NRP was built by cross-functional teams involving more than 500 employees in three months and the fact that more than twenty new or completely updated vehicle models were created in just two years—light speed considering the pace at which Nissan previously had moved. Problems have arisen along the way after the alliance and will continue, as with any company. But Nissan has kept its torrid pace by responding to trouble as quickly as it plans and implements.

"If a problem surfaces, it is expected to be put on the table immediately," says Norio Matsumura, a member of the executive committee. "In the past, we tried to put off the problem. Today, we are encouraging everyone to put it forth immediately so we can solve it."

Commitment

The most important word in Nissan's key-term English dictionary is the one most used by executives and managers. They have given new meaning to the word "commitment," ingraining it in everyday use so much that it has become a corporate cornerstone of promise and achievement.

Commitment has certainly been a part of business efforts large and small all over the world before, but perhaps no company has used it as extensively and effectively as Nissan. From the key-word dictionary:

"Commitment is an objective to be accomplished. The objective to be accomplished is demonstrated by numerical values, and pledged. Once it is committed, it has to be achieved except for extraordinary events. In the event that the objective is not accomplished then one has to be prepared to take the consequences."

A more practical definition is this: A commitment is a personal promise from executives and managers to Ghosn that set objectives will be met. For example, an executive commits to selling 3 percent more cars in a specific area and he is expected to deliver or pay the price.

An hour spent with an executive—any executive—finds

the term used over and over again, making it the key to all business at Nissan: commitment to the company; commitment to setting higher standards; and commitment to Ghosn. In other words, when Ghosn changed Nissan's scheme to direct responsibility for all employees—including him—the term commitment took on great importance within the company because it is the promise they make as to what performance and results they will deliver for each quarter, half year, and full year.

"Commitment is now a key proposition at Nissan," one manager says, completely aware of the understatement he made.

Ghosn set the standard for commitment when he said during the NRP announcement that he and other executive committee members would quit if Nissan was not profitable within a year. He was asking a company—a country—to reform, but he put his own neck on the line in doing so, making public commitments that he and fellow executive committee members were accountable for. In a similar manner, he gets executives and managers to make commitments to him and these promises are taken seriously like nothing else within the company.

The notion immediately comes to mind that all large companies do this, making periodic projections they must stand by. This is obviously true. But there is a different quality and seriousness about Nissan's "commitment" and the personal promise to Ghosn that goes along with it.

"It was difficult to accept this concept in the beginning," says Tadao Takahashi, an executive vice president of manufacturing. "We were 'committed' and we were 'challenged,' but these did not coexist. Little by little, people have changed. Now we understand commitment."

•　•　•

Ghosn hates vagueness; absolutely cannot stand it, in fact. Therefore, employees know that when they go before him with a problem, a solution, or to make quarterly or annual projections, they must be careful not to imply that something can be done or he will consider it a commitment made. Ghosn is well known for his ability to convince employees they can reach goals they ordinarily feel are unattainable. Executives and managers tell stories about walking into his office for a meeting about a problem and leaving afterward, scratching their head, realizing they have just made a commitment that is by all means expected to be kept.

"At first, nobody understood what this meant, commitment," Viadieu says. "People never committed before. They were responsible for nothing."

Viadieu laughs at the memory of going before Ghosn to seek help with a problem, only to be given a sensible, but complex, solution. "He explains and you say to yourself, 'Yes, I get it. I am so stupid.' Then, you go back to your office and say, 'No, now I don't understand.' He makes it sound so simple but it is not. You have to be very careful what you commit to because he expects you to deliver."

Commitments Made Must Be Kept

Executives and managers are told that unless immediate notification of trouble is given, the commitment is expected to be on track. If problems develop, teams are put together to solve the problem in the quickest manner possible to keep the commitment on track. The executive committee reviews "critical" commitments every month and works immediately to find solutions if promises are not being met.

How serious is Ghosn about commitment? One example is what he told the general manager of the professional soccer team Nissan owns. The F-Marinos, based in Yokohama, play in the Japan League and are wholly owned by Nissan. Ghosn, an avid soccer fan from his days in Brazil, was adamant during Nissan's sale of noncore assets that sports investments, such as motor sports and soccer, were off limits, due to their brand-enhancing ability. Nissan actually increased its stake in the F-Marinos in 2001 from a majority holding to 100 percent ownership.

"When I came, people thought I would be cutting everything, including sports," he says. "Now in Japan other companies are cutting sports activities. We, in fact, are spending more. We are reinvesting . . . because building motivation is so important."

In return, Ghosn, who oversees the F-Marinos as part of his "administration for affiliated companies" role as CEO, acquired a couple of new players to help the soccer team in 2002 and got the coach and general manager to "commit" to finishing in third place during the regular season. There are fifteen teams in F-Marinos' division. In 2001, they won just nine games and finished in thirteenth place out of the fifteen teams, yet Ghosn received a commitment to finish in at least third place before the 2002 season.

Carlos Ghosn is all about commitment.

Why?

"Because Nissan is the owner of the team and the F-Marinos have many fans," he says. "I don't want them to be a bunch of soft players reflecting poorly on Nissan . . . I want them to be under pressure to perform. It's important that in everything you do, people give their best."

The F-Marinos, remarkably, were in first place in their division halfway through the season and Ghosn says he noticed a major difference from the previous year when he did not challenge them with a commitment. "They are proud of the improvement because they like the interest we show in them," he says. "In a way, they are happy about the added pressure."

Target

As if making the commitment and meeting it is not enough, the next word of importance from the key-term dictionary is target, Ghosn's favorite. Executives and mangers commit, they reach the objective, and then comes the stretch, in an effort to get to the target.

From Nissan's key-word dictionary: Targets are goals higher than committed objectives; targets are not committed, but it is better if they are achieved.

Nissan executives and managers know that reaching the commitment—the promise—is a necessity if they are to be considered performing at reasonable levels. But they know that to excel, they must be continually striving for, and more than occasionally meeting, the target—the optimal goal for each reporting period.

Thus, the word target is synonymous with commitment.

Ghosn even applies it when talking about the F-Marinos: "They are in the target," he says with a smile. "We are hoping."

Outside of the soccer team, the target is serious business for Ghosn and others at Nissan, though it isn't viewed with the same measure of absoluteness as the commitment, for obvious reasons. Meeting and exceeding targets—stretching beyond what seems reasonable when commitments are made—has been a signature of Nissan's revival effort and the reason the NRP and other reform measures have been achieved before allotted time. And consider that since Ghosn has pushed the Japanese executives and managers to commit at high levels, the targets that are subsequently set are often ultra-aggressive.

For example, core NRP goals, to be achieved in three years, like the 20 percent reduction in supply costs, were commitments. And loose ones at that, considering many within the company in November 1999, just one month after the NRP was announced, were still having to be convinced through daily meetings that it could be done. Ghosn made stops to floors beneath his fifteenth floor office to meet with department team members in efforts to convince them what their immediate superior could not: it could be done.

That the NRP was concluded in just two years and many of the original goals exceeded meant that most targets were met or exceeded, giving way to the next part of Nissan's complete invigoration effort, NISSAN 180. This is serious business in Japan, where forecasts by many executives and managers tend to be soft so that goals can easily be met. But that is exactly why Nissan reacted so slowly in the past and Ghosn is not interested in a repeat performance. He insists they commit higher so targets will mean something.

"Mr. Ghosn is always challenging us to make higher commitments and targets," Tadao Takahashi says. "We [constantly] talk about challenge and stretch."

Nissan's six program directors, responsible for overall sales and profitability of specific models, are constantly discussing progress and problems with every product so targets can be reached and plans don't fall off course. Shigeru Sakai, a program director who has been called "the Infiniti guy" around Nissan for his efforts in Nissan's U.S. luxury line of vehicles, says every business issue at Nissan since the alliance is a "matter of how far we can stretch it," unless consumer quality is involved.

"Commitment and stretch—two of Ghosn-san's favorite words," he says, smiling.

Itaru Koeda, a veteran Nissan employee and a member of the executive committee, isn't shy about saying the commitment-stretch-target scheme has pushed people at all levels of the company to go beyond basic requirements, especially those at the top.

"After [Ghosn] joined Nissan, every employee worked harder," Koeda says.

Managing People

Ghosn is accurately portrayed in the media as a man with above-average intensity. He approaches every subject and issue with focus and desire, leaving no doubt he wants whatever is at stake done properly. When you watch him work or talk to him you can see it and feel it in every move he makes and every word he says.

Make no mistake: Carlos Ghosn is an intense man.

But there is no evidence within Nissan, or Japan, for that matter, that Ghosn is a man who loses his cool, even occasionally. To the contrary, Ghosn is said by others to be a man who is always consistent with those he works with, never showing displays of yelling and desk-pounding, which other intense CEOs have been noted for. Ghosn is intense but reasonable when dealing with people. He challenges them, but empowers them with trust, not harsh words.

"I'm not a micromanager," he says. "When I trust people, I let them do their job."

Ghosn uses his analytical instinct to determine the strengths and weaknesses of others, pushing hot buttons he determines makes them work harder. "He has an ability to look into the people," says Tomii. "If we are talking about a candidate for a particular position, he can see directly into the good points of this person. If we are looking at one of our dealers, he can look into the head of the outlet in a very limited time and determine the strengths and weaknesses very quickly."

While others can feel Ghosn's intensity while he speaks, he rarely, if ever, explodes while offering direction for the company. Instead, he deals with people in a pragmatic way, conveying his demands for success with focus. "I'm a tense person," he says. "I try to keep it inside."

Ghosn works at turning his intensity and lack of patience into management strengths that tie directly into the company's urgency, driving the fact that tomorrow is too late to do what needs to be done into the minds of employees. "The day I'm not useful to the company, they'll find many weaknesses in my style," he says.

So far, most are following, not questioning, their leader. Ghosn, in fact, earns seemingly profound respect from many older, veteran managers who appreciate his fresh approach to running a company and the way he has made their jobs interesting and challenging once again. Kiyoaki Sawada has worked at Nissan for more than twenty-five years. He and Ghosn are the same age but Sawada considers his boss to be younger because of his aggressive and energetic manner. "He gives me opportunity to challenge myself," Sawada says.

Jim Morton's history and relationship with Ghosn is unique in itself for two reasons. He was one of the executives hand-chosen to follow Ghosn to Nissan and he and Ghosn share a genuine friendship. Ghosn, the 7-11 CEO and father of four, has little time for hobbies or friendships outside of family and work, so his lasting bond with Morton has significance.

Morton first met Ghosn in 1989. He was director of public relations and public affairs for Michelin North America in Greenville, South Carolina, when a young Carlos Ghosn was named president of Michelin's North American division. Government and public relations played an important role in the company's acquisition of Uniroyal-Goodrich, making Morton one of Ghosn's top problem-solvers during the fast-moving times at Michelin in the 1990s. Morton is more than eight years older than Ghosn and accomplished himself, holding a law degree and a corporate career to be proud of with stops at the likes of Arthur Andersen and General Dynamics. Still, he considered Ghosn a role model from the start, and that has not changed today.

"I look up to Carlos Ghosn," Morton says. "I may be older than him, but I've always considered him a mentor. He is a new international executive . . . the world has never seen anything like it. We could see that when he came to Greenville and he was still in his thirties then."

When Ghosn left Michelin for Renault in France in 1996 he kept in contact with Morton, who remained at Michelin. Ghosn maintained his residence in Greenville and called Morton when he came to town, and Morton, by then a vice president at Michelin North America, visited the Ghosn family in Paris periodically when he traveled to France for company business.

"We would break bread together," Morton says, noting that even then he was one of a rare few allowed in the inner space and time Ghosn reserved for family.

It was during one of these visits in 1999 when Ghosn suggested Morton join him at Nissan. "I told him immediately I was interested," Morton says. "I knew [Nissan] was a challenge and told him I thought it would be fun. I had seen him work for years and knew he would get the job done."

Morton did not get the job on the spot, even though the suggestion was made by Ghosn. Nissan's new leader did not want to shove executive personnel down the throats of other company executives, particularly key Japanese leaders already shaken by Ghosn's fast-paced style and blueprints of change. Norio Matsumura interviewed Morton for the job.

"He said to me, 'I'm not sure why we are doing this,'" Morton says, chuckling at the memory. "I told him, 'That's just how Carlos Ghosn works. He isn't going to do this if you don't buy in. He knows it will never work if you do not agree.'"

Making Tough Decisions

Nissan is strengthened because Ghosn empowers employees at all levels by gathering information and creating levels of cross-work teams but the big decisions are always in the office of the CEO.

Ghosn uses the information he gathers from others as his foundation for decisions, which are typically fact-based and deeply calculated. He looks, he listens, and he appraises. Then he acts in the manner he believes is best according to the factual information he was given.

"Very rarely does he resort to political thinking," Klein says. "Basically, his decisions are fact-based, and profit usually comes first as the motive."

Deciding to go for the NRP at the maximum reform levels he believed were possible is one example. Objectives were set from information and recommendations gathered within the company. When it was time to make decisions, some executives suggested the company not go for all changes at once, grandfathering in the most radical moves. Ghosn admits to giving pause over the drastic measures he was considering, particularly the plant closings and job reductions in Japan. He is a family man before he is a businessman and the thought that thousands who relied on Nissan could be without work was unsettling. He listened to what others had to say and considered his vision for the company.

"He goes around to many departments and listens to many voices," Watanabe says. "He gathers this information for input, but he makes the final decisions."

Ghosn ultimately went for it all against the advice of others at the company because he believed restoring profitability and confidence in the company was imperative to Nissan's survival. More jobs could be created worldwide long-term through short-term suffering that restored profitability and trust in the company.

"It was a tough call," he says, "but there was so much expectation to deliver results . . . the only thing I could not do was not deliver."

Ghosn uses the same practice when final decisions are made regarding design and engineering of the dozens of new models Nissan is bringing to market. It is well documented that Ghosn loves cars and has the final say in design decisions at Nissan, to the point of actually giving specific vehicle aspects a thumbs up or down based on personal beliefs. But he bases these decisions on automotive knowledge and beliefs, not personal tastes, since models that may suit his personal flavor may not sell well in a particular region.

"I have always liked cars," Ghosn says, "but I am not a car nut. A car manufacturer has to make money. I may decide to go with a car I don't like if it is good business for the company."

Also, the size of the investment does not determine how much time is spent gathering information. Once the facts are in, the decision at the top is made. "As long as the logic is sound, he will make the decision [to proceed]," Shiro Nakamura says. "Time and money are not related and that is very unusual for a CEO. He is quick to come to the focal point in design proposals and he is able to make a decision."

Consistency

The lack of management consistency that plagued Nissan before is not evident now, as the man at the top makes a daily effort to bring the same face to the CEO office every day. Ghosn sticks to the company's objectives and speaks in the same manner, every day, in contrast to the stereotypical Japanese company president who says something should be done only to change his mind the next day, bowing to pressure from others.

And it is really no different in America, where companies launch plans but detour before they are complete because management is on another hunt. Speaking change is one thing. Doing it is another. Ghosn wants to be a predictable leader because he says employees find strength in consistency. Therefore, he works at showing the same mannerisms and style at the office and follows up what he says with corresponding action.

People have had enough of leaders who do not think, say, and do the same thing.

It is easier to get away with leading in erratic ways when times are good economically. In Japan in the 1980s executives could do no wrong; same with America in the 1990s. But bubbles that burst and markets that deflate give way to uneasiness among consumers, employees, and shareholders. Leaders at the top can soothe fears and give comfort simply by walking the lines they talk. They can also give those within the company confidence to make decisions themselves that follow the predictability of the CEO.

"Consistency in management is something people are expecting in difficult times," Ghosn says. "They like you to be a little predictable. In a certain way, it empowers them to make decisions because they know exactly how you are going to react."

If people have no idea how a manager or executive will respond to a decision, they are not comfortable with making. If the person at the top is predictable, they know their decision fits with standard operation and they tackle the issue themselves. The predictability empowers the people and the CEO's strength extends far beyond his top-floor office.

CHAPTER NINE

How to Achieve World-Class Status

Saying out loud in 1999 that Nissan would have a legitimate shot at becoming one of the strongest and best automakers in the world just a few years later would have drawn blank stares, maybe even a few snickers.

Survival, possible.

Mediocrity, maybe.

Record profits and award-winning cars, no chance.

Few would have dared to imagine the impossible, much less share it with anyone familiar with Nissan and the hurdles it faced. Even Carlos Ghosn did not talk about such thoughts when he arrived at Nissan because the company was in such bad shape he knew his management authority would be weakened, if not lost, by such dreamy talk. When this notion of Nissan becoming a world industry leader was finally voiced early in 2002, Ghosn had two years of record results behind him, making the possibilities conceivable. There were still doubters, as with the NRP, but credibility in making such a statement was no longer an issue. Nissan's managerial philosophy of "do as you say" paid off.

The Nissan Revival Plan, designed to restore profitability and growth at a company that had been dormant for a decade or more, contained three major commitments. The second and third commitments were achieved one full year ahead of schedule, culminating with a record-breaking earnings report.

- Management committed in 1999 to returning Nissan to bottom-line profitability in the first year of the NRP and it was done.
- Management committed to achieving an operating profit margin of 4.5 percent by the end of the fiscal year 2002 and by the end of fiscal year 2001, Nissan reported a margin of 7.9 percent, on par with Japanese competitors Toyota and Honda.
- Management committed to reducing net automotive debt in half to no more than 700 million yen while increasing the company's investment rate from 3.7 percent to 5 percent of sales by the end of 2002.

  Twelve months ahead of time, at the end of fiscal year 2001, Nissan's net automotive debt stood at 435 billion yen, the lowest it had been in twenty-four years.

The NRP accomplished yet more:

- The automotive production parts supplier base was reduced by 40 percent, while service suppliers were reduced 60 percent.

- Five plants were closed, resulting in an increase in manufacturing utilization rates from an average of 51 percent before the NRP to a level of 75 percent at the end of FY 2001.
- Manufacturing platforms in Japan were reduced from 24 to 15.

But the NRP only put Nissan back on the map. It did not give the company significant advantage over its competitors because, due to the ailing financial shape of the company in 1999, the sterling results of the NRP, while a dramatic turnaround, only put it on a par level with other world automakers. It showed with the design of products like the all-new Z car and the restyled Altima that it could create consumer excitement. But to be one of the world's most efficient automakers Nissan had to be able to grow, profitably, over a sustained period of time.

To determine how this long-term dream could become a reality Ghosn looked once again inside the company for the answers. The same cross-functional teams that were used to draw up the NRP, with some new players and different and additional subteams, investigated, discussed, and proposed more ways Nissan could achieve lasting profitable growth. The result was NISSAN 180, the plan designed to make Nissan a world leader in the automotive industry.

During the NRP phase of revival, Nissan focused on returning to profitability, sacrificing all market shares that did not put positive numbers on the bottom line. Ghosn said he didn't want any market share the company did not earn and let it go without a second glance. Through NISSAN 180, launched in April 2002 (the beginning of the company's 2002 fiscal year), the emphasis shifted from short-term profitability to long-term profitable growth—the secret to lasting success.

"There's no more doubt that Nissan can be profitable," Klein says. "The capability to grow is another story. We have to demonstrate we are capable . . . outside, people are skeptical still because Nissan did not grow for a long, long time. The only way to convince them is to deliver."

THE MEANING AND OBJECTIVES OF NISSAN 180 (TO BE ACHIEVED BY THE END OF FISCAL YEAR 2004):

"1"—stands for an additional one million unit sales worldwide by the end of fiscal year 2004 compared with fiscal year 2001.

"8"—stands for an 8 percent operating margin, a figure that would put Nissan consistently at the top level of profitability in the global auto industry.

"0"—stands for zero net automotive debt

Doubters surfaced soon after the NISSAN 180 plan was announced, and some inside the company were scratching their heads, similar to the days after the NRP was unveiled. Several executives and managers displayed broad smiles and funny looks when asked about the aggressive objectives of NISSAN 180. A few even shook their heads when asked about the plan's rule-the-automotive-world nature. It wasn't a look of "this can't be done" panic. One just got the feeling they knew the size of the challenge ahead, fresh off two years of hard-working revival efforts.

Ghosn is experienced with this type of trepidation and admits NISSAN 180 is more aggressive in reality than the NRP because large-scale growth is always difficult for old, established companies. The objective that Nissan would sell one million more units in three years was intimidating considering that at the end of 2001, when the new plan was announced, global unit sales were totally flat compared with the previous year, even declining a fraction. That some people openly bristled at a worldwide unit sales increase of 40 percent in three years is understandable. People in general want to gauge the size of a challenge by what they did or did not do before, Ghosn says.

It is human tendency to look at the past to determine the future.

But NISSAN 180 was built on factual analysis using data and insight that says achieving the stated goals is possible if the company hits on all cylinders in all corners of the world it conducts business.

TOTAL UNIT SALES:

2001–2,597,000 (actual)

2004–3,600,000 (projected)

"When we said we would bring Nissan back to real profitability the first year, people said we'd never make it," he says. "We did. For the moment, people are saying NISSAN 180 can't be done. But we are not in the past. The one-million-unit increase is not a careless shot from the hip. It has been analyzed market by market. Until it's done, sure, it's natural, it's fair to question. But the last three years, we established a track record and we are intent upon continuing on the same track."

Norio Matsumura is perhaps the Nissan executive under the most pressure to perform in NISSAN 180. His duties as the head of the company's global sales and marketing effort make him responsible for seeing that one million additional units are sold in 2004, compared to total sales in 2001. Matsumura is a hard-working, personable type who has worked at Nissan for more than twenty-five years. He says the added pressure is totally different from how it was in the past but makes it clear that the new environment and challenges have made work interesting and invigorating.

"Now I've got to sell one million more vehicles," he says, broadly smiling. "It's my 'mission impossible.'"

Matsumura quickly adds that he is making a joke and that reaching the objective is possible because the pipeline of innovative products is already developed and sales and marketing activities are beginning to run effectively on a global scale, building Nissan's brand image.

"It can be done," he says. "It is achievable."

NISSAN 180 RELIES ON FOUR PILLARS:

- more revenue (through one million additional unit sales)
- less cost (reducing costs 15 percent over three years)

- more quality and speed (focusing on product and management)
- maximized alliance with Renault (finding synergies that benefit both)

More Revenue

Nissan's global market share at the end of fiscal year 2001 was 4.7 percent. The aim of NISSAN 180 is to grow unit sales by almost 40 percent over three years, resulting in global market share of more than 6 percent. Ghosn, saying the dramatic increase would "not happen easily or automatically," believes that the fact that Nissan has planned for the growth "methodically" and in a "disciplined manner" ensures it can be done.

The map for growth consists of the following breakdown: 300,000 additional units in Japan (17.9 to 22.5 percent market share); 300,000-plus in the United States (4.2 to 6.2 percent); 100,000 in Europe (2.5 to 3.1 percent); and 300,000 in the general overseas markets.

Nissan plans on driving the increase in volume through new products and new market development. The company will launch "a minimum of twenty-eight all-new products" worldwide during the three-year NISSAN 180 plan and set specific market goals. For example, Ghosn wants Nissan to have at least three models ranked in the top ten best-selling vehicles in Japan. He also wants the company to "significantly" improve its customer and sales satisfaction index scores in the United States.

Most of the work was done on the new products in terms of design and planning during the NRP, but the company only started to see benefits at the end of fiscal year 2001 (which ended March 31, 2002) when the first vehicles hit the market. The impact, similar to what Nissan experienced with the Altima, the Infiniti G35 sedan at the end of 2001, and the 350Z sports car (sold as the Fairlady Z in Japan), the restyled Maxima, and the all new Murano sports-utility vehicles in fiscal year 2002, is anticipated to be significant and part of what Ghosn calls Nissan's "broad-base product offensive."

Nissan also aims to push sales by continuing to enhance its brand power, a process started through the NRP. The company set objectives in improving its brand power and closing the resale value gap it has with competitors and increasing customer satisfaction ratings by using a familiar technique that has worked well in purchasing: benchmarking.

Ghosn said Nissan's brand power and resale value, while improved, was still below that of competitors like Toyota in Japan and the United States and Volkswagen in Europe and that both companies were selected as benchmarks by which NISSAN 180 objectives were set. Nissan aims to reduce the transaction price and resale value gap with Toyota by 50 percent; and with Volkswagen by 30 percent. Increasing consumer belief that Nissan offers innovative and quality products is how it will be done.

Internal surveys from the early 1990s showed that in 1991 Nissan placed four models among the top ten most innovative cars in Japan according to consumer belief. By the mid-1990s, Nissan models had totally disappeared from the top ten. By 2000, 42 percent of the people surveyed described Nissan as an innovative company versus a 70 percent return for the leader, Toyota.

"We need to change this perception back and for Nissan to be viewed as innovative," Ghosn said.

Nissan plans to grow its general overseas markets—sales areas outside of the major operations centers in Japan, Europe, and North America—by increasing its presence in developing countries where automobile demand is high, like China. The Asian country plays such a significant role in Nissan's quest to sell one million more models by the end of 2004 that Ghosn split China responsibilities from the general overseas market group, assigning one of his Japanese "young turks"—an identified up-and-coming company leader—to tackle the new task of overseeing and growing China operations.

Katsumi Nakamura, who played a key role in the development of the full-size truck as a program director, reports directly to Ghosn in his new role, one of the more challenging in the company considering the market is essentially new for Nissan. The company's presence in China began in late 1972 with imports of Cedric sedans but was limited to several joint venture agreements that racked up sales of just 25,000 units in 2001. Nissan began exploring much larger-scale operations in China shortly after it was announced that Nakamura would be in charge of developing sales in the country and the public learned of the company's aggressive sales growth plans through NISSAN 180.

Nissan and China's DongFeng Automobile Co. Ltd. agreed to establish a 50-50 joint venture and will grow the company into a full-time car company based in China. Nissan and DongFeng already had a joint agreement to manufacture pick-ups, a commercial truck, and one car model. But it was nothing in comparison to the new, full-scale agreement which gives

Nissan a shot at catching up to rivals like Honda and Toyota, which currently have a large presence in China.

The country is seen within the auto industry as one of the hottest growth markets existing and Nissan believes that China can play a major role in helping Nissan reach lofty growth plan goals. The China market is booming after years of dashing the hopes of the world's largest automakers. Passenger-car sales jumped 18 percent in 2001 and were up 37 percent in the first five months of 2002. That's welcome news for Nissan, which is launching its aggressive growth plan in the midst of a sluggish car market worldwide.

Other automakers are already heavily invested in China since arriving in the 1980s and have been waiting for salaries to rise and car sales to jump in the country. Ghosn says Nissan is behind its Japanese rivals who entered the China market sooner, but believes the company will make up lost ground within four years by delivering innovative and affordable products to China that are manufactured domestically. He says the sudden market surge is not likely to stop any time soon and says China will play a large role in Nissan's future growth.

"It's true that in China we were late, but we were late everywhere," he said.

Less Cost

Nissan promised suppliers in 1999 that those helping the company reach cost-reduction objectives would be rewarded with more business. The number of suppliers would be reduced, providing those left with more existing business, and additional sales volume would reward survivors of Nissan's purchasing reform.

Suppliers were given a NISSAN 180 ultimatum similar to the one they were given at the start of the NRP: Purchasing costs must be reduced at least 15 percent over three years. The difference this time was that Nissan was launching twenty-eight all-new products during NISSAN 180 compared with nine during the NRP. NISSAN 180 specifically targets unit sales increases while the NRP did not. Ghosn says it is easier to reduce cost on new vehicles than existing ones, for obvious reasons, allowing Nissan to contribute more to the cost reductions than it previously did.

"I know from my past experience as a supplier how much growing volumes and a renewed product lineup can support increased competitiveness and profitability," he said.

Nissan is helping suppliers by increasing its contribution to cost reductions through its "3–3–3" activities. The engineering department, as one example, contributed 33 percent to the effort under the NRP but is increasing that amount to 50 percent in NISSAN 180. Still, Nissan is aware that helping reduce costs doesn't always inspire suppliers to do so with a smile. Ghosn says telling them how it will be doesn't always work. In other words, rationale does not make motivation.

That's why Executive Vice President Itaru Koeda has worked hard at convincing suppliers that Nissan only "closed the gap" on competitors through its NRP cuts and that the company is determined to "move ahead." He says suppliers who are cooperating in finding cost-saving solutions will thrive with Nissan, while those that do not will suffer, ultimately having to look elsewhere for business.

"To move ahead of our competitors we must do this," Koeda says.

The relationship between a manufacturer and a supplier should be viewed creatively on both sides, Ghosn says. He uses his experience on the supply side in the tire industry to his advantage with the automaker, understanding that they will offer deeper cuts when the manufacturer takes an active role in finding solutions.

"The limit of savings that can be squeezed from the supplier chain is your imagination and your ability to help suppliers reduce their costs," Ghosn says. "A lot of people look at the relationship between a manufacturer and a supplier as a static relationship—the manufacturer asks for a twenty percent cost reduction and the supplier responds yes or no.

"But what happens is that the manufacturers set the objective and then discuss with the supplier how to eliminate waste and cost from the system. There is no limit to this process, as long as you are doing it fairly. You must be ready to challenge yourself as much as you challenge your supplier."

Nissan is reducing operational costs in the areas of manufacturing and global logistics (12 percent) and distribution (3 percent). The company will also eliminate almost all of its finance costs as the net automotive debt rolls toward zero, allowing research and development costs to remain steady, creating the opportunity to increase investments by entering new markets, and facilitating the ability to strengthen sales and marketing areas.

More Quality and Speed

Finding ways to generate more business at less cost has been a cornerstone of Nissan's revival, but the company will not reach its ultimate goal of lasting profitable growth without emphasizing to a greater degree the quality of its products and the management and speed with which plans are implemented.

The problem with launching so many new models so fast is that quality must be ensured so that consumers will tell others about the products and will want to buy from Nissan again in the future, Ghosn says.

Quality is a company's single most precious asset.

Nissan launched a new program called "Quality 3-3-3," which focuses on three categories of quality: product attractiveness, product initial quality and reliability, and sales and service quality. The program, which runs concurrently with NISSAN 180, aims to position Nissan products among the top three in each category in each region, or at the least to be the "best Japanese make" in a specific market, like the United States.

Management quality will be determined by surveys that will be conducted three times per year. The surveys will "ensure that management is in tune with company and employee expectations." Ghosn says the best management practices occur when "values and performance can be quantified and measured."

V-Up Teams Formed

Carlos Ghosn's signature management tool and a cornerstone of the emerging "Nissan way" are undoubtedly the cross-functional teams, which played such an important role in the NRP and the formulation of the NISSAN 180 plan. The CFTs will continue throughout implementation of NISSAN 180, offering broad solutions to management on issues ranging from finance to purchasing. But Nissan launched another layer of problem solvers to its middle management line by establishing the Value-up program.

Known within the company as V-up, the program utilizes more than 400 "V-pilots" in a manner similar to how CFT pilots function, with the exception that V-up pilots will typically have smaller teams and more specific areas of focus. V-pilots began training in 2002, shortly after NISSAN 180 was announced. Their challenge is to offer continuous process improvement and field-level problem solutions.

The V-up program, just like the CFTs, is a part of Nissan's "the answers can be found within" philosophy that empowers middle managers by giving them freedom to actively find problems and recommend solutions. The CFTs challenge the company by addressing high-level "strategic and structural issues" and proposing possible solutions at the upper management level while V-up teams are a tool for management to improve processes and efficiency by solving specific problems. V-up teams are given a specific task from management and expected to come up with a concrete solution to resolve the issue through cross-functional work in a relatively short time period.

Ghosn doesn't believe in stifling employees who run the company every day, choosing instead to relieve the boredom and frustrations that typically strike middle managers in Japan with empowerment to fix and lead the company by providing solutions to everyday problems. They are the ones who can immediately determine if specific processes need improvement. By the time small problems reach the office of the CEO they have become big problems.

The Renault Nissan Alliance

The alliance between Renault and Nissan is unlike any other ownership agreement between major corporations anywhere in the world. This is not a dictatorship and it is not a partnership. It is a unique union between companies seeking to maintain separate identities while finding increasing ways to benefit from joint synergies and the sharing of ideas at all levels.

It is an isolated French company and an emerging Japanese company working together in a binational manner to find more customers and higher profits in a global context. Granted, it is unusual for one automaker to pay billions of dollars for controlling-share ownership of another that was struggling, to devote countless other resources to its revival effort, and not to demand that its imprint be placed all over the company it saved, but that is exactly how Renault has approached its alliance with Nissan.

Schweitzer made it clear he believed Renault and Nissan would benefit the most if both companies maintained separate brand and corporate identities, merging instead the best each had to offer in terms of strengths and weaknesses. Ghosn reinforced this concept in his early days at Nissan when he stressed time and time again that he and others were at Nissan for the good of Nissan, not for the good of Renault. The belief was that as Nissan strengthened, Renault would strengthen based on its ownership and expanded global exposure.

Finding behind-the-scenes synergies that benefited both companies was the focus from the start as the cross-company teams that functioned before the alliance was signed continued to explore ways Renault and Nissan could work together. Specifics, like the Renault Nissan Purchasing Organization, which was formed in 2000 to shave additional costs of parts and supplies that both companies used, and joint manufacturing arrangements like the Renault cars being built at Nissan plants in Mexico, began to emerge in public view during the NRP, reinforcing the importance of the alliance to Nissan and Renault.

Nissan needed a partner when it was struggling in the late 1990s because it could not solve its problems alone. Renault was the answer. Ghosn says the alliance helps Nissan "go beyond performance" it could achieve alone. "It is a significant advantage," he says.

Both companies, though, need each other in every feasible way if they are to grow substantially in terms of market share and profits in the coming years, because of the increased clout and market exposure they offer one another. The companies combined to sell more than five million vehicles per year, placing Renault-Nissan among the top six car manufacturers in the world. The best part is that they are strong in different markets, offering extensive future piggybacking opportunities. That's why Renault invested in Nissan initially, because it was largely confined to European market share. Nissan is strong where Renault is weak or has no presence at all and vice versa. That's also why the alliance and resulting synergies continue to grow beyond what first occurred when the alliance was signed in the spring of 1999.

The most significant change came when Renault exercised its options that were granted in the agreement, increasing its ownership stake in Nissan to 44.4 percent. Nissan also increased its ownership stake in Renault to 15 percent in May 2002.

Ironically, concern was voiced by market investors when it was first speculated that Nissan would exercise its right to obtain ownership in Renault because as one company was strengthening on the heels of its aggressive revival plan the other was showing profit decline, a victim of difficult conditions in the European market and an aging product line of its own. Renault reported a 77 percent drop in operating profit to EUR473 million in 2001, from EUR2.02 billion a year earlier. The company's auto division posted an operating profit of EUR216 million, or less than 1 percent of revenue, last year.

Ghosn says no further moves are planned for the future and that shareholding moves by both companies were allowed and called for in the alliance document signed by Hanawa and Schweitzer and it only makes sense for them to execute options.

The alliance is based on "mutual trust and respect" and an agreement that is "very atypical" in comparison with other unions between automakers and that the particular aspects of it make following it to the letter important for both companies. "This cross-shareholding arrangement is nothing new," Ghosn says. "It was part of the agreement signed in March of 1999 and we have to follow it scrupulously so that we maintain trust."

Ghosn says it is natural that any time you have two companies the size of Renault and Nissan in an alliance there will be "obvious frictions, emotions, and suspicions" but that typically these are overcome by action and results on both ends. "The balance is one of performance," he says.

The type of ownership involved is not what is important to partners of an alliance. It is all about performance on common projects on both sides.

The alliance will focus during NISSAN 180 on three main directions: marketing and sales to derive a common approach in specific markets such as Mexico, South America, and North Africa; generating more efficiency through selective finding of common ground in areas such as platforms and powertrains (while allowing each brand to maintain distinct product identities where consumers are concerned); and extensive exchange of the best practices in all areas of business between the companies.

Specific issues and objectives are studied and appraised by eleven cross-company teams that focus on such areas as product planning and strategy, powertrains, engineering, purchasing, manufacturing and logistics, and markets where one of the two allies has a strong presence. The CCTS are in turn supported in daily work by nine functional task teams. The CCTs and FTTs are supported by an Alliance Coordination Bureau (CB), which has offices in Paris and Tokyo to facilitate communication and implementation on both ends. The Global Alliance Committee (GAC) became the governing body of the alliance. Now called the Alliance Board Meeting (ABM), it meets monthly to review specific projects presented by the joint operational teams (CCTs) and give guidance and authorization when needed. The International Advisory Board serves a broader need, providing advice and recommendations as to the evolution of the alliance, but it does not get involved in operational specifics.

A top to bottom explanation of how alliance cross-fertilization between Renault and Nissan works is this: the CCTs study and appraise, submitting proposals to the ABM. The CCTs are provided in-depth research and backup support by the FTTs. The ABM makes decisions on submitted proposals and each company implements through follow up from CCTs. The result is a layered cross-fertilization plan that breeds increasingly more areas and ways in which the companies can save money and grow by working together.

Bernard Long, vice president of international human resources, is also charged with facilitating communication between the companies, which occurs primarily by way of the eleven CCTs. His job is to "enhance maximum transparency" on each subject while helping to instill a global view that is reflective of core values at both companies. His advantage is having worked for both. Long moved to Nissan shortly after the alliance because he liked the lifestyle Tokyo offered.

"From time to time we are pushing, other times we are pulling, trying to facilitate brainstorming between the teams," Long says. "Cross-work is a key element: cross-company, cross-functional, cross-fertilization. Nissan is the benchmark in manufacturing, but Renault is offering the ergonomic aspect."

"Of course facilitation is easier said than done," he says. "When something does not go correctly it is quickly famous within the company."

Long is one of more than thirty expats working at Nissan

in Japan at the beginning of NISSAN 180. Others in France volunteer routinely to make the move, hoping to benefit from Nissan's momentum and the safe, easy pace compared with the bustling atmosphere they experience in Paris. Their children ride the subway at night in Tokyo to meet friends and find entertainment. In Paris their children need adult supervision to ride in a taxi.

RENAULT NISSAN ALLIANCE KEY DATES

1999

- The Renault-Nissan agreement is signed (March 27).
- Yoshikazu Hanawa joins Renault's board of directors (June 10).
- Carlos Ghosn is appointed chief operating officer of Nissan (June 25).
- The Nissan Revival Plan is announced (October 18).
- Renault's return to Mexico with Nissan support is announced (December 9).

2000

- The International Advisory Board is created (March 30).
- The plan for developing Renault's presence in Japan with support of Nissan is announced (April 25).
- Nissan's decision to develop its activities in South America (Mercosur) with the help of Renault is announced (May 29).

- Carlos Ghosn is appointed president and COO of Nissan (June 20).
- Renault Scenic production starts at Nissan's Cuernavaca, Mexico, plant (December 6).

2001

- Renault and Nissan announce the joint development of a second common platform (for C segment vehicles) in addition to the first common platform (for B segment vehicles) under development since 1999 (February 7).
- Renault and Nissan Global Purchasing Organization is set up (April 2).
- Renault products are launched in Australia with Nissan support (May).
- Renault's comeback in the Indonesian market with Nissan support is announced (June 13).
- Carlos Ghosn is appointed president and CEO of Nissan (June 21).
- Renault Nissan BV, which steers alliance strategy and joint programs, is established (October 30).

One of the more interesting aspects of the alliance is the way Nissan has been at the forefront from a public perspective, stealing headlines around the world for its underdog-turnaround success story while Renault rarely gets mention or credit in the accounts. Nissan comes to life and Ghosn is named Auto Executive of the Year—in France. The irony is obvious, considering that Renault was in fact Nissan's savior. But Schweitzer and others at the French company left egos out of the equation at the start, Ghosn says. They happily let Nissan take its high-profile perch during its revival effort, while continually work-ing through cross-company teams to offer more support, glean-ing what they could in return.

The story is no different internally. That fact becomes clear when talking to groups of French and Japanese about the alliance from the perspective of top-level management. The French—Ghosn included—talk frequently about Schweitzer and his role in having the courage to create the alliance and take a chance on Nissan. It's only natural since Schweitzer was the expats' most recent boss and they still have ties to Renault even though they draw paychecks from Nissan.

"Let's not forget that Mr. Schweitzer was brilliant," Viadieu says. "He made the alliance happen. He hired Mr. Ghosn at Renault and he sent Mr. Ghosn to Nissan. You can't compare those two because they are two completely different people, but together they make a nice combination."

Many Japanese see Ghosn as their gift from the alliance. They see him as the man who taught them to think and work differently and aren't shy about saying so. "Nissan gets many things from Renault but the biggest is Mr. Ghosn," Sawada says.

CHAPTER TEN

Boldly Going in New Directions

The best way for a company to shake its stale image and convince consumers it is on the innovative edge is by going in directions it has not dared before.

Nissan's calculated risk-taking has become a signature of its revival effort and the boldest moves will likely have the biggest impacts on the company, in terms of products and capital investments. Simply put, the boldest moves have the biggest risks and the most at stake in terms of Nissan's ability to achieve lasting profitable growth.

A drive down Interstate 55 through hot, humid central Mississippi in the summer of 2002 reveals a centerpiece of the company's new direction in North America, its conviction to become a risk-taking world leader instead of a Japanese conglomerate follower. The stubborn, rural Southern landscape suddenly gives way to an enormous white industrial oasis spreading over hundreds of acres and nested directly up to the eastern side of the interstate highway that splits Mississippi in half like a zipper running head to toe. The only color one can see besides the massive splash of white from the new plant: Nissan, written in red across the new water tower built for the plant.

The company stands out in Mississippi already.

Gov. Ronnie Musgrove has just returned from a visit to Japan, where he met with Ghosn and members of Nissan's executive committee as well as a handful of major suppliers who are considering locating in Mississippi to support Nissan's new facility. He has good news about the plant, which is still under construction but is scheduled to open in May 2003. Nissan's billion-dollar investment, which created such a stir in Mississippi and among its 2.5 million residents, is going up almost a year before the first car is scheduled to roll off assembly lines. Nissan's original plans, announced in November 2000, called for a $930 million investment and 4,000 jobs. The design called for an E-shaped facility to be built, allowing for future expansion by closing in the E. Nissan said at the time it hoped to add production to the facility, but Mississippi leaders believed it would be sometime after manufacturing had begun. The company's aggressive plans under NISSAN 180, in which the U.S. market plays such a vital role, contributing an additional 300,000 units sold per year by the end of 2004, sped up the schedule.

The Canton, Mississippi, plant will be expanded with another $500 million Nissan investment and 1,300 more jobs, raising production capacity to 400,000 units from the 250,000 called for in the original plans. The expansion is needed so Nissan can add production of the Altima to keep up with exploding consumer demand. Nissan can't make its 2002 North American Car of the Year fast enough. The Smyrna plant will make 225,000 Altima sedans in 2002, exceeding line capacity by more than 25,000 units, and it isn't enough, because more could be sold and more need to be sold. Nissan will start making the Altima in Canton in 2004, producing 150,000 units per year. The Altima will still be made in Smyrna, but the reduced load lets the company add production of another vehicle there in the future.

"We are working overtime to build the Altima in Tennessee and we are still not meeting demand," Emil Hassan says.

Nissan will also build a new Quest minivan at the Canton plant (a restyled version of the vehicle, which was formerly built in the United States through a vehicle-sharing agreement with Ford), the all-new full-size pickup, and both an Infiniti-brand and a Nissan-brand sport-utility vehicle. The company's total investment commitment in Canton increased to $1.43 billion with the expansion, which will force Nissan to add another one million square feet of floor space to the plant, bringing the total space to four million square feet. In addition, the company will have to build a second paint plant. The paint plant under construction in Canton was designed for the larger trucks, vans, and sport-utility vehicles that had been planned for the plant. More important for Mississippi, the expansion will create 5,300 high-wage jobs, significant in the state where per capita income was $20,993 in 2000—dead last among the fifty states and almost $9,000 below the national average.

Musgrove, thrilled that Nissan will build one of its best products in the state, called a special summertime legislative session to ask the Mississippi House and Senate to approve an additional $68 million in incentives ($23.5 million for worker training; $22.5 million for road, water system, and other infrastructure improvements; $12 million for site preparation; and $10 million for a vehicle preparation facility) in return for Nissan's second-phase plant expansion in Canton. Mississippi had already guaranteed $295 million of incentives, bringing its total to $363 million.

Legislators overwhelmingly approved the package by a margin of ten to one, rare in a state that is almost always politically divided when it comes to government spending. Musgrove is sure Nissan is worth every penny.

"I am reminded of it every time I drive by," he says. "The structure makes a dramatic statement. It broke the barrier of disbelief in Mississippi."

The expansion comes at a time when the state is embroiled in another controversy, hitting right at the heart of Nissan and other large manufacturing companies. Mississippi was targeted by the national U.S. Chamber of Commerce as one of the worst states in the country to do business because of its unfriendly legal system, which rewards plaintiffs with handsome jury awards. The tort reform turf battle is so severe that many major insurance companies have pulled out of Mississippi and major businesses have publicly said to change or they will take capital investments and go elsewhere. Nissan is taking a different approach, continuing its investment but believing that as one of the state's most significant industries it can create change in the place that needs "meaningful reforms" when it comes to tort issues.

Nissan is already creating change in the state in other ways. The small town of Canton, which has a dated central business square and too few jobs, is already perking up. One of the biggest days Canton had seen before came in the late 1990s when John Grisham's *A Time to Kill* was filmed downtown and movie stars, extras, and onlookers flocked to the area. Now, improved roads and schools are only the beginning of the change that is occurring and lies ahead. Mention Nissan around town and, typically, you get a smile.

That Nissan came to central Mississippi is not an accident. Millions in incentives and the quick response Mississippi offered were enticing, but three other qualified sites offered incentives to the company as well. Nissan looked straight in the face of those who whisper in manufacturing corners that Japanese companies don't like to locate in areas with large minority populations because they don't like working with African-Americans, and chose Mississippi for the new plant. It's typical of the new style at Nissan, taking bold action and avoiding vague words and promises.

We won't just talk about diversity, we'll show you diversity.

Nissan committed to hiring a workforce reflective of the citizenry of Canton and surrounding areas of Mississippi. The company, which lists the Canton plant as a diversity asset on its website, saying it will have a major "social and economic impact" on the state, donated a million dollars to fund scholarships in the state and financially supports historically black, private Tougaloo College in nearby Jackson. Ghosn and executives at Nissan North America actively talk about the potential they believe exists to create long-term change in one of the nation's poorest states by creating an economic spark that lights a social fire.

The governor agrees that people's lives will be different. "Ten years from now we will look back and say that when Nissan arrived is when our state made a tremendous turn," he says.

A Full-Size Gamble

The risks involved with launching an entirely new vehicle are directly related to the physical size of the model, designer Shiro Nakamura says. Bigger bodies have bigger risks, making Nissan's full-size truck, which will be built at the Canton plant, a full-size challenge.

"It's a very American domestic product," Nakamura says. "We carefully maintained the basic requirements for a full-size, U.S.-built truck. Then, we put our own taste of innovation on it. It is more like a sports car to me . . . it is aggressive and very emotional, making it fun to drive."

The American full-size pickup truck-buying public is typically a conservative bunch, buying products built by different manufacturers that have little design differentiation. Nissan wanted to offer consumers an alternative.

To be bold, it had to be different.

The result was a truck that conjures up thoughts of something that could be ridden by a space cowboy, if one existed. He wears a hat. He hauls a load. He does it all riding a sleek, mechanical horse with strange powers. "We put our dreams into the full-size truck," says Katsumi Nakamura, who helped develop the truck in his previous role as program director. "We took a cowboy hat concept and put it into Japanese technology and engineering."

Consumer focus groups that were shown models of the truck during development gave Nissan exactly the response it is looking for when bringing such a dramatic product to market. "They love it or hate it," Katsumi Nakamura says. "That's a very good result for us."

Nissan isn't expecting to put the Big Three out of the truck business. The goal is just to offer existing customers more options to stay within the Nissan family when they look for additional models and begin building a base of new customers who like alternatives when shopping for a new vehicle. "We are after the type of customers who are passionate about what they do and active minded," Katsumi Nakamura says.

Hiring Once Again

Nissan is also after the hearts and minds of consumers by showing it has changed through its bold action and new products. The goal is not just to have a hit truck, but to have a hit truck that reinforces Nissan's emerging image as an innovative automaker. The goal was not just to build a flashy small car (March) in Japan that would sell, but to build a car that would sell and show through its innovative colors and amenities, like on-board e-mail, that it is a company thinking ahead for a change. The work appears to be paying off. Two years after closing plants and eliminating jobs the company is hiring again.

Top young guns avoided Nissan during its old case of corporate complacency, preferring instead to work for hot companies like Sony and Toyota. Nissan was dated and traditional and considered a corporate graveyard by youngsters who commit to the Japanese job for life upon graduation. Now, the company is on the move, advertising its job openings with a "join the movement" type of campaign. Sharp young people are coming back. One Nissan employee said the company hired arguably its best class of college graduates ever in 2002 during the annual spring hiring season, proof that the message is being heard.

That Nissan is hiring at all is a miracle of sorts. The company announced in 2002 it was increasing its worldwide staff by about 3 percent, to 129,000 employees, by the end of the fiscal year in March. It is the first time since the alliance Nissan has increased its staffing levels. Almost 500 new college graduates joined Nissan's Japan operations in the spring and more than 500 midcareer workers were expected to join the company, including some former employees, bringing the revival effort full circle in a short time.

The company also talking about renovating corporate headquarters buildings in Tokyo's plush Ginza district. Money spent on facility renovations—outside of manufacturing—during the NRP was strategically planned, going to places where an innovative look and feel was the most important, like the technical center where vehicles are designed.

A couple of state-of-the-art, public-vehicle showrooms were also built in Japan. One is on the ground floor of one of the headquarter buildings; the other, just down the street on one of Tokyo's most visible and expensive street corners. The showrooms, with a futuristic look and feel, are popular meetings spots in the bustling neighborhood for businesspeople and visitors stopping in for coffee and to see and touch Nissan's latest models. Upstairs, offices filled by administrative staff were nice and comfortable, but the décor was dated to a period when Nissan was at its prime in Japan—the mid-1970s. Renovations were delayed until the results were in, but plans for improvements were being made just as the NRP was coming to an end.

In the United States, the company began hiring the first of its anticipated 5,300 factory workers for Canton, and a $39 million expansion of the Nissan Technical Center North America was announced, including more than 260 "high-wage, high-skill engineering and technical positions." The technical center, located in Farmington Hills, Michigan (just outside Detroit), is Nissan's North American research and engineering facility responsible for vehicle development. The technical center includes an arm of Nissan Design America in San Diego. Design director Tom Semple says Nissan is hungry for new and experienced talent to meet increasing production demands and a hectic work schedule. He says the pace is only quickening and that designers and engineers at the U.S. centers have been working to meet model growth needs for Infiniti and Nissan lines during the revival period. The new hires will find a challenge and rarely a dull moment, helping Nissan strive toward its goal of becoming the leading and most efficient automaker in the world.

It will not be easy. To get the job done and meet commitments, they will have to jump into the fire like others before them. They can benefit from Nissan's global cross-communicative, team support approach and experience that others had meeting targets during the NRP. But to excel and push Nissan closer to its ambitious targets, they will have to be bold.

CHAPTER ELEVEN

One Man Makes a Difference

Many tactics and techniques were used to transform Nissan from a loser into a winner in just three years' time, but the turnaround would not have occurred without extraordinary vision at the top.

Carlos Ghosn is a man who follows facts and reason, not conventional and stereotypical wisdom when it comes to people and places, allowing him to see Nissan and Japanese business traditions differently than others. Conventional wisdom said that none of what has happened during Nissan's three-year rocket ride should have happened. When Renault acquired control of Japan's beleaguered automaker, global observers predicted a disastrous clash of cultures. Japanese do business in specific, traditional ways and do not like foreign interference. Besides, stereotypical wisdom says that Japanese manufacturers do not hold their European counterparts too highly.

So Ghosn arrives from France to run the show; he can't speak the language and needs a lesson in the proper use of chopsticks. He is going to change the company and world business along the way.

Talk about trouble.

Chalk up another victim to the empty promises of globalization.

Nissan was a formidable company with a significant worldwide presence in 1999 despite its financial troubles, but Renault was the only company willing to take the expensive risk. The others apparently could not get past what seemed obvious: Nissan was broke and the Japanese people would not change. It is unlikely that many people were thinking that Ghosn was a global visionary when he moved his family to Tokyo.

In Japan there were whispers of *"Ghosn the gaijin"* at first, a moderate reference to the foreigner attempting to turn around the company that was once the corporate crown jewel of a proud country. Soon, though, they were boasting of *"Ghosn-san"* (Mr. Ghosn) and reading a comic series about his heroic efforts by the hundreds of thousands. Some have become so charged by his reform abilities they want him to save Japan's struggling economy next: *Ghosn-san the gaijin, prime minister of Japan.*

There is a natural resistance people have to giving one person too much credit for success when throngs of others are involved. It goes against logic and personal comfort to say out loud "she changed the world" or "he saved the company." Certainly, *surely*, others were involved. No one person is bigger than a company, no one persona bigger than all the others combined.

And so goes the case at Nissan, the company that raced

from hell to purgatory and got a glimpse of the heavens in just three years' time. Thousands of people were involved in the remarkable revival—almost 130,000 to be exact—and the stories of individual and team successes from Tokyo to Los Angeles to Smyrna are abundant. But big business thrives on strong and timely leadership, and in this case, vision. Nissan was a company in 1999 caught in perpetuity. It was not profitable and had fragmented, and in some cases weakly supported, operations around the world. Cries for help came from all over but nobody—not one single person—was successfully doing anything about the problems that were destroying the company.

Nissan was not struggling because of low employee morale or poor capital investments. These were by-products of much bigger problems. It was a global company with a regional mind-set, a manufacturer without a product or profit cause. The company was bigger than the people; the people bigger than the person.

Carlos Ghosn saw it. And he was not afraid to change it.

He arrived with a multicultural, energetic flair, thinking complex and talking simple. First, he looked for answers within. Then, he gave Nissan employees a bigger view of the company and its place in the global market in ways they had not seen or heard before and could not help but follow. It made all the difference in the world and turned an ailing company into an industry leader.

"Maybe only Carlos Ghosn could have saved Nissan at that very moment in 1999," says Emil Hassan.

Hassan, a top Nissan North America executive, may draw his paycheck from Nissan but he is known for his outspoken, direct style and only says what he believes is true. He is an all star in an industry of egos who says the match of Ghosn and his talents with Nissan and its unique troubles was a perfect corporate fit.

Nissan's Smyrna, Tennessee, manufacturing plant, located just thirty miles outside of Nashville, was already known as the most efficient in the country, if not the world. But Hassan, a Nissan veteran of more than twenty years, was planning to leave the company because he was tired of ongoing management problems stemming from poor communication in Japan. He met with Ghosn during the "clean sheet of paper" tour in 1999 and says what he saw in Nissan's new leader made him know the company would never again be the same.

"I saw this ability in Carlos Ghosn in the first hour we met," he says. "So there was no decision for me to continue my career at Nissan. He got a lot of input [on the tour], but it was his sharp focus and quick decisions that made the difference and created real change. He is so intuitive."

"I have always been a believer that one person can make a difference," Hassan says. "I know some people don't like to think that, but I know this is true. Carlos Ghosn is a perfect example of how one person can create drastic change. He did it making practically no personnel changes. It was the same company. He was the difference."

It is unusual for even insiders to point such a strong finger at one individual, including the CEO. Publicly, maybe. Off the record, when their guard is down and true feelings are revealed? Rarely.

Jed Connelly, Nissan's highest ranking North American sales and marketing official, was through with his interview and headed out the door, late for another meeting, when he paused for parting words. The writer had already put his pen down and closed his notebook. Pleasantries had been exchanged. Connelly is a sharply-dressed, middle-aged man and a seasoned automobile industry executive who has been around, having done upper-level management stints at Volkswagen and Sterling Motors in North America, among others.

He had been talking about Nissan and Ghosn for more than an hour during a scheduled interview in which he was upbeat but reasonably guarded in his words. But on the way out the door, he wanted to add something. His facial expression changed. His eyes were wide open now; his voice a whisper. It felt like he was about to unleash a secret.

"You know," he says, "sometimes I sit back and think to myself . . . someday I am going to be sitting around watching television with my grandchildren and something about Ghosn is going to come on. I will be telling them, 'I know that man and had the privilege of working closely with him for a while.'"

"I know that I am part of something big at Nissan," Connelly says. "But I also know that I am getting the wonderful chance to witness something bigger . . . and that's Carlos Ghosn."

They try and put a finger on exactly what it is, the difference in a visionary and a lucky man. They talk about Ghosn's simplicity, how he works at making the complex understandable. They talk about his clarity and obsession with always getting it right, whether it is a one-paragraph internal memo or a new car design.

There is no room for error.

None.

Whatever it is, there is clearly something about his style that makes even outsiders know something different is going on inside Nissan and that the catalyst of change is Ghosn.

One analyst said DaimlerChrysler would likely gain $10 billion in market-capitalization during one day of trading if Ghosn were named CEO of that company. Another industry insider compared him to basketball star Michael Jordan, saying he is "changing the game" of international business. Even Robert Lutz, the former Chrysler executive now at General Motors, said publicly while he was the CEO of battery-maker Exide that the turnaround at Nissan might not have happened if not for Ghosn and his radical ways.

Not everybody loves the job Ghosn has done, naturally. A small handful of Japanese journalists have been periodic thorns, claiming he is taking the Japanese heart and soul out of a traditional Japanese company. Others have criticized him for not learning Japanese customs quickly enough. He once missed an important function attended annually by Japanese suppliers. Another time he was chastised for not bowing properly at a shareholders meeting.

Ghosn's response is that his actions at Nissan are preserving a Japanese company, not killing it, and that he has worked so hard since arriving in Japan that he has had no time to learn all the customs. But, he adds, "I'll do better."

Frankly, Ghosn is hard to criticize. It is even difficult finding someone else to criticize him outside of those in Japan who accuse him of taking the Japanese out of the company because he operates daily on the "transparency" mode, hiding behind nothing that is obvious. When Nissan stumbles, he is the first to admit it. And his multicultural, nonstereotypical style makes caging him in a corner virtually impossible.

It was evident at the end of just a few months on the job—specifically the moment he sent the NRP off like a rocket with his shot-heard-round-the-business-world speech—that Ghosn is a different type of leader and someone whom most people at Nissan want to hold on to as long as is reasonable. It became impossible for those inside the company or out to talk about Ghosn and Nissan without speculating about what future job he might take. Even Nissan executives did not talk about Ghosn in interviews without bringing up the subject, unprovoked. It was as if they knew the question was coming. And it probably was.

Public speculation about Ghosn's future was at its highest in 2001 when Nissan was turning heads with its dramatic results from the second year of the NRP. Members of the media, in typical fashion, did not just speculate, they asked point blank: "Have you been approached to take a job at any other automaker?"

Ghosn gave the quintessential response for an executive supposedly looking beyond his current position. "This is becoming a classic question to which I will give the classic answer," he told the *Automotive News* in an interview. "I consider my mission is to help put Nissan on track for lasting profitable growth, and nothing will divert my attention from that."

It would have been easy for anyone to draw the conclusion, reading that response, that Ghosn will simply do what any typical chief executive or football coach does who turns a loser into a winner: He'll turn the company around and get out as fast as he can, just as it peaks.

But Ghosn is not your typical chief executive or turn-around expert.

There was speculation that one option for Ghosn would be to return to France and replace Schweitzer, who was hinting at retirement. After all, Ghosn and his family had just moved into their newly renovated, sixteenth-century "dream" home in Paris when he accepted the Nissan job and moved the family into an apartment in Tokyo. Returning to Renault would make sense, except for the fact that by the time Nissan finished the second part of its revival, the company would be much larger than Renault, making the move a parallel one at best.

Then the news came: Ghosn will likely become the CEO of Renault in 2005 when Schweitzer semiretires and moves to chairman of the board. And the kicker: Ghosn will likely also remain CEO of Nissan.

"I'm not sure I need to be replaced at Nissan," said Ghosn, who was named to Renault's board of directors in the summer of 2002. "You could imagine a scenario where you have one CEO for two companies."

If the scenario plays out that way, Nissan and Renault would each have chief operating officers, responsible for day-to-day operations. Both companies would be under the direction of Ghosn, who would hold a seat on Nissan's executive committee and a seat on Renault's board.

"A lot of people worry what happens to Nissan after Ghosn," he said. "After Ghosn is going to take a long time. After Ghosn is not 2005."

Two companies. Two languages. Two continents.
And one trailblazing CEO.

Not exactly what one would have expected, but typical of the atypical alliance between French Renault and Japanese Nissan in which business is not conducted according to rules set by others.

Typical of Carlos Ghosn, as well.

CHAPTER TWELVE

A Complete Turnaround

The final chapter in Nissan's two-phase quest for world automotive excellence will not be written for two more years, when the second of its two revitalization plans comes to an end, but the story already has the makings of a happy ending.

The Nissan Revival Plan restored hope, profits, and confidence in the company. NISSAN 180 is designed to create lasting profitable growth, placing the company well above competitors in terms of profit margins and consumer satisfaction. If Nissan succeeds, reaching its lofty objectives of achieving zero net automotive debt and one million additional units sold per year, it will become the industry's benchmark standard instead of the company setting benchmarks by others.

Only time will tell if NISSAN 180 commitments and targets are reached. But the question of Nissan's revival—its com-

plete turnaround, from near disaster to corporate cover-boy—
has already been answered, loud and clear.

The company's Japanese employees accepted Ghosn's
challenge and learned new ways of working, reaching across
disciplines and continents in a cross-functional, hard-charging
spirit like never seen before inside Nissan. When they say yes,
they mean it; when tough decisions have to be made, they are
not delayed.

The French stuck to their original commitment of allowing both companies to grow and mature as allies while maintaining separate brand and corporate identities. Certainly,
Nissan and Renault are moving closer with each passing day, as
talk of Ghosn serving as CEO of both companies at once
proves. Hanawa, already, has been a dual board member; now
Ghosn. There may be others in the future. And the companies
announced in the summer of 2002 that they were finding more
ways to benefit from synergies.

Renault and Nissan enhanced the scope of their joint purchasing company by raising annual volumes to around $21 bil-
lion from $15 billion. They also launched a new joint venture,
Renault-Nissan Information Services. The RNIS is designed to
add "value to Renault and Nissan's respective operations by
boosting performance and reducing costs" in an area that
Ghosn sees as crucial to the future of the alliance. The RNIS is
headquartered in Tokyo with a branch office in Paris, a flip-
flop of the global purchasing company, which has headquarters
in Paris and a branch office in Tokyo; just another small sign in
the unique nature of the always evolving Renault Nissan
Alliance.

The North Americans continued doing what they do best:

designing, manufacturing, and selling cars efficiently and profitably, setting the global standard for other Nissan operations. But the North Americans also did something else. They ignited from sparks given off by the alliance and Nissan's enhanced global, communicative network. They found new markets and boldly searched for others. The Z-car is back and better than before. Infiniti has a full range of new products and the full-size truck is about to roll off the lines of a new $1.4 billion manufacturing facility sitting in the heart of one very thankful Southern state.

Together, the people of Nissan followed a vision of renewed spirit and global cohesion, removing physical and cultural boundaries that existed from Europe to Asia to North America. The result is a diverse, Japanese-based company that meets the true definition of globalization. They set out to revive the company but did a lot more. New cars are designed with the best of ideas from different regions in a cross-functional manner. Communication plans are drawn up with one brand and identity in mind. Human resource schemes are being integrated and centralized, reflecting corporate, not regional, standards.

The tangible successes are many even though the revival at Nissan has only been underway for just over three years. Nissan posted its most profitable years in the company's history and proved it can design and build exciting new products in a short amount of time. And this: Nissan stopped the string of consecutive years the company lost market share in Japan dead in its tracks at twenty-seven.

It is true that restoring profitability can be easier than growing at profitable levels for sustained periods of time.

That's why eyes are upon the company and its attack of NISSAN 180, the new plan of promise. The objectives set are far more aggressive than those in the Nissan Revival Plan and its boldness, which caught a country and an industry completely off-guard. The nonbelievers do not number as many as before but they still exist, doubting whether Nissan can go from average to excellence in terms of profits and consumer satisfaction.

So questions remain as to exactly how high and how far Nissan will go in its ultimate quest. Only time and results will tell. But the final assessment of the original goal set by Ghosn and Renault—the rescue of Nissan—has already been made, revealing one, clear conclusion.

Renault took a chance. Ghosn went to work. And Nissan responded.

Together, they changed world business forever.

Notes

160   "Cadillac Eldorado," *Wall Street Journal*, December 27, 2001.

160   "Bingo," *Wall Street Journal*, December 27, 2001.

231   "Have you been approached to take a job . . ." *Automotive News*, December 17, 2001

231   "This is becoming a classic question to which . . ." *Automotive News*, December 17, 2001